Women of Dutchess County, New York: Voices and Talents

Part I

Dutchess County Historical Society
2020 Yearbook • Volume 99

Candace J. Lewis, *Editor*

Dutchess County Historical Society

The Dutchess County Historical Society is a not-for-profit educational organization that collects, preserves, and interprets the history of Dutchess County, New York, from the period of the arrival of the first Native Americans until the present day.

Publications Committee:

Candace J. Lewis, Ph.D., *Editor*

Michael Boden, David Dengel, Dennis Dengel,
John Desmond, Roger Donway, Eileen Hayden,
Bill Jeffway, Melodye Moore, Elizabeth Strauss,
William P. Tatum III Ph.D. and Andrew Villani

Designer: Marla Neville, Main Printing, Poughkeepsie, New York
mymainprinter.com

Dutchess County, NY Printer: Main Printing, Poughkeepsie, New York
mymainprinter.com

Dutchess County Historical Society Yearbook 2020
Volume 99 • Published annually since 1915
Copyright © by Dutchess County Historical Society
ISSN: 0739-8565
ISBN: 978-0-944733-15-8

Cover: Top: Amenia Field Day, August 1913, Photograph. White-clad suffragists march at the Amenia Field Day in August 1913. Amenia Historical Society Digital Collection. Bottom: Woman Suffrage pageant during the Amenia Field Day at Troutbeck, 1914. Amy Spingarn collection, Amenia Historical Society Digital Collection.

Back cover: Left: Caroline M. Clowes, Two Cows at Wappingers Creek, titled by the artist, signed "C.M. Clowes, 1882." The Dutchess County Historical Society, The Caroline M. Clowes Collection, Gift of Linda and E. Stuart Hubbard, 2019.

Middle: Dr. Josephine Evarts at her Millerton office late in her career. Photograph. Bob Kristofik, Poughkeepsie Journal.

Right: Billboard promoting woman suffrage, 1917. Collections of New York State Library, Manuscripts and Collections, Albany NY, SC23360, USGEN-94. "We are ready to work beside you, Fight beside you and Die beside you—VOTE FOR WOMAN SUFFRAGE November 6th.".

The Dutchess County Historical Society Yearbook does not assume responsibility for statements of fact or opinion made by the authors.

Dutchess County Historical Society
P.O. Box 88
Poughkeepsie, NY 12602
845-471-1630
email: contact@dchsny.org
dchsny.org

This issue of the Dutchesss County Historical Society's yearbook has been generously underwritten by the following:

Anonymous

Anonymous

David Dengel

Dennis Dengel

We support our women of Dutchess County.

Joan Smith

In loving memory of
James R. Smith (1946-2016)

Shirley M. Handel

LTC Gilbert A. Krom

In memory of a beloved brother
and fine soldier.

Lou and Candace J. Lewis

F. Julius and Carla Gude

❧

Martin and Eleanor
Rubin Charwat

Elizabeth and Julian Strauss

Roger and Alisan Donway

Poughkeepsie Public Library District
is proud of its longtime association with the Dutchess
County Historical Society. Together we offer our community
a selection of exciting avenues into our fascinating past.

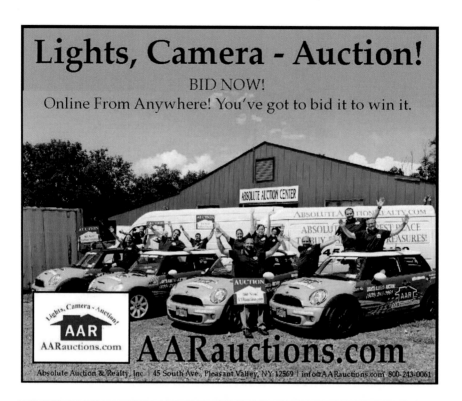

In Memoriam

Richard C. Strain (September 17, 1932-April 4, 2020)

Richard Strain died at home in Poughkeepsie this April at the age of 87 years old. During his life, Richard, who was known to his friends as Dick, was a local businessman, athlete, sportsman, and philanthropist.

Dick attended Clinton School, Poughkeepsie High School, and Philips Exeter Academy. He graduated from Yale University with a Bachelor of Mechanical Engineering in 1954 and a Bachelor of Science, Business Administration in 1955. After graduation, Dick returned to Dutchess County to work for his father at C.B. Strain & Son. He married Anne Parks and they had four children. Dick took over the company at his father's death in 1975. His daughter, Karen, would take over as President in 2009. The business was sold in 2012.

In the community, Dick was well known for his athletic accomplishments. He loved sports and played with pleasure, always encouraging others. At the Poughkeepsie Tennis Club, he won the Men's Singles Championship a record 13 times over a 15 year period. He liked to say that he could have been "really good" if he had been born to be left-handed and 6 feet 4 inches tall. Golf was also a favorite and he was an excellent player, winning many tournaments.

Later in life, Dick devoted more of his free time to the life of a sportsman. He was an avid fly fisherman, seeking out interesting places to visit all over the world. Dick is also remembered for his support of local not-for-profit groups. He has been a staunch supporter of the Dutchess County Historical Society. He has supported Planned Parenthood of the Mid-Hudson Valley, the Community Foundations, and local artists.

He is survived by his four children and eight grandchildren: Teddy Mulrow, her husband Bill and their children Kelly, Jennifer, and Jack; Karen Smythe, her husband Nevill and their children Ryan and Dennison: Linda Hillery, her husband Matt and their children Daniel, Margaret, and Katherine, and John Strain; and final companion Nancy Rubsam.

In Memoriam

The Reverend F. Kennon Moody
(July 9, 1933-April 11, 2020)

F. Kennon Moody, died at home in his sleep at the Fountains in Millbrook, New York on April 11. He was 86 years old. Ken was a Methodist minister, a master story teller, a teacher, an historian, and author.

Ken was from Cotton Valley, LA, the youngest of four children. He graduated valedictorian of his high school and attended Centenary College in Shreveport, LA, earning a B.A. in history. Then he went north to New Haven, CT to the Yale Divinity School where he received a Master of Divinity in 1958. He married Mary Law and they moved to Williston, VT, where Ken became pastor at the Federated Church and both of their children were born.

In 1963, Ken and Mary moved to LaGrangeville, NY, where Ken served as the pastor of the Trinity United Methodist Church. While at Trinity, Ken worked with a group of parishioner to launch Dutchess Rural Housing Corp, a non-profit that built homes for low-income families. Ken left Trinity Church to join the South Forty Corporation, a non-profit to help prisoners and recent parolees. From then on, he spent his career in extension ministry. He taught history at Dutchess Community College and, while there, obtained his Ph.D. in American History with a dissertation on Franklin D. Roosevelt.

Ken remained passionate about history in his later years, acting as a professional researcher on Roosevelt and assisting other writers. He authored FDR and his Hudson Valley Neighbors. He contributed to more than a dozen books and a PBS special. Ken also took a strong interest in the story of abolition and Black rights in America, writing on the topic. He was a contributor to the Dutchess County Historical Society yearbook.

He is survived by his son David, his daughter-in-law Eileen Guilfoyle and their two children, Sophie and Gus, as well as by his daughter Laura Hoskins, her husband Dan, and their two children Min Ho and Madeleine. His wife of sixty years, Mary Law Moody, died March 28, 2019.

In Memoriam

Robert J. Murphy (1948-2020)

Beacon City Historian Robert J. Murphy, son of the late Robert W. Murphy and Elizabeth Murphy, passed away after a courageous fight with cancer on July 10, 2020. A 1966 graduate of Beacon High School, he earned a bachelor's degree from Manhattan College and a master's degree from the State University of New York at Albany. Bob served as president of the Beacon Historical Society (BHS) for 20 years (1998 – 2018). He wrote the popular BHS monthly newsletter for 38 years and co-authored two books, *Historic Beacon* and *Beacon Revisited*. He was working on his third book at the time of his death.

Bob possessed an encyclopedic knowledge of local news events, families, and changing streetscapes; he selflessly devoted his life to finding and celebrating Beacon's history. His gift to all of us was his love for his hometown and his unwavering commitment to share its past. He prepared dozens of presentations and contributed numerous articles about Beacon's history throughout the decades. In 2015, Bob was the recipient of the Dutchess County Historical Society's prestigious "Dutchess Award," recognizing his exceptional contributions as a local historian. In 2019, he was honored at the Beacon Historical Society's Third Annual Beacons of History awards.

In addition to his love of history, Bob was an avid reader, writer, bread baker, photographer, gardener and woodworker. In his younger years, Bob was a talented baseball player and skater, who loved playing hockey beside his nephews. For the past 38 years, he and his sister, Diane, enjoyed daily walks and hikes to Mt. Beacon, Denning's Point and other points around Beacon. He taught himself to develop negatives and made thousands of prints for the BHS archives.

Bob and his great sense of humor and gentle, quiet ways will be greatly missed by his family, friends, and community.

Table of Contents

FORUM: Women of Dutchess County, NY: Voices and Talents, Part I

ARTICLES: Miscellaneous Topics in Dutchess County History

ADDENDA

Letter from the Editor

In 2020, we celebrate the hundredth anniversary of the 19th Amendment to the United States Constitution giving women in this country the right to vote. This issue of the Dutchess County Historical Society Yearbook is dedicated to remembering the efforts leading to that moment.

In the 1840s, Elizabeth Cady Stanton and others were organizing in her home town the signature event that would mark the beginning of the Woman Suffrage Movement in America. At that time, most married women in this country could not own property, could not control their money, could not divorce their husbands if they wanted to, nor could they have access to their children without the consent of their husbands. Also they could not vote. Finally, we should remember that a large part of the population, both female and male was still held in slavery.

The Seneca Falls Convention held in upper New York State in July of 1848 drew approximately 300 participants. Led by Elizabeth Cady Stanton and Lucretia Mott, this group did not yet include Susan B. Anthony, who would soon work hand in hand with Elizabeth Cady Stanton and then become leader of the movement in later years. It did include a black man, Frederick Douglass. The main goal was to discuss methods for obtaining social and political rights for women. Woman suffrage was not yet central to the mission. Nevertheless, that meeting would be the start of a more than 70-year-long effort of meetings, teas, and marches to win the vote for women.

By the early years of the twentieth century, many states, most of them in the West, were passing state amendments allowing women to vote. New York State did so in 1917.

In 1900, Carrie Chapman Catt succeeded Susan B. Anthony as the head of the Woman Suffrage Association. In 1914, Carrie Catt launched an effort to link her movement to the United States war effort in World War I. Therefore, women's suffrage would be portrayed as patriotic. This proved to be a brilliant move. Many canning parties and ladies' patriotic marches later, her effort was a success. In his 1918 State of the Union Address to the Nation, ramrod stiff President Woodrow Wilson reversed his earlier opposition to Woman Suffrage and declared his support of women's right to vote. After this, the amendment was on the road to final passage.

The 19th Amendment begins…

> The right of citizens of the United States to vote shall not be denied or abridged by the United States or by any state on account of sex. Congress shall have the power to enforce this article by appropriate legislation.

The 19th Amendment to the United States Constitutionwas ratified on August 18, 1920. It was certified by the U. S. Secretary of State Bainbridge Colby on August 26 of that year. On November 2, 1920, 8 million women in the United States voted in elections for the first time. It took over 60 years for the remaining 12 states (that had not already done so) to ratify the 19th Amendment. Mississippi was the last to ratify---on March 22, 1984.

Thus, in New York State in the early part of the nineteenth century, a few women and men were keenly aware of injustice in their world and had begun calling for change. At the Seneca Falls Convention, the group issued a Declaration of Sentiments modeled on the Declaration of Independence. It began with the statement, "We hold these truths to be self-evident; that all men and women are created equal." So, in 1920 with the Ratification of the 19th Amendment to the Constitution, the right to vote was secured for the women of the United States.

As per our usual practice, we have divided the book into two sections, the Forum section with a major theme--- Women of Dutchess County: Voices and Talents, and an Articles section with essays on topics of general interest in local history. In our thematic section for 2020, we have 10 essays, four of them on the subject of women's suffrage. In addition, in the remaining essays we have highlighted the achievements of local women in various fields of endeavor, including art, law, ecology, health, medicine, and the environment. In the Articles section, there is an essay about a twentieth century photographer from Beacon.

As always, we want to thank the authors for their contributions and our donors for their support. We could not produce this book after 105 years without you. Please note: the article by Bill Jeffway on recently rediscovered painter Caroline M. Clowes is especially important to the Dutchess County Historical Society. We have been researching this artist intensively and plan to exhibit her story and work both online and at the Barrett House.

Also, I would like to draw the reader's attention to the article by Myra Armstead on the Flu of 1918. We are presently in a very difficult period as we deal with the coronavirus pandemic. Looking back at a similar time in history gives us perspective. We wish everyone safety and good health.

— Candace J. Lewis, Ph.D., editor

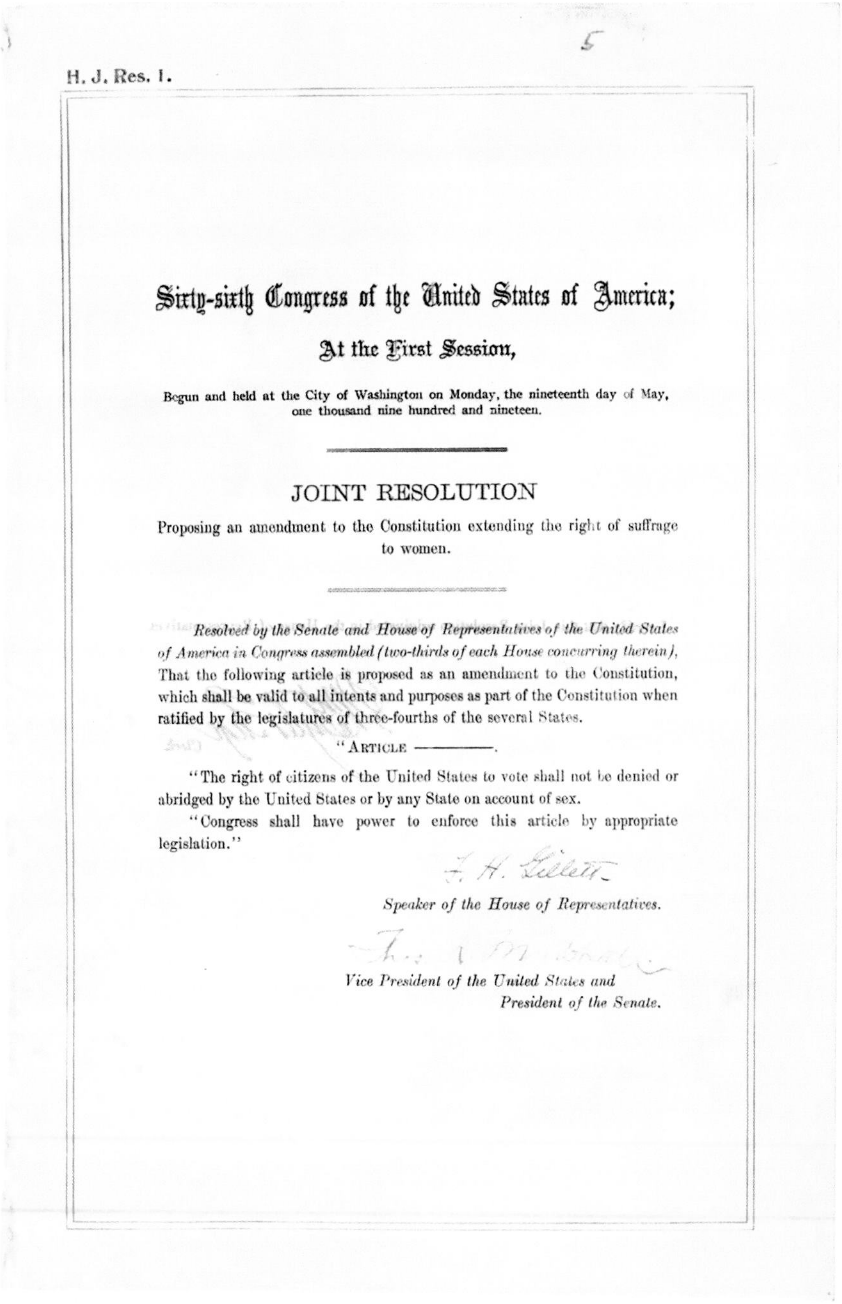

5

Sixty-sixth Congress of the United States of America;

At the First Session,

Begun and held at the City of Washington on Monday, the nineteenth day of May, one thousand nine hundred and nineteen.

JOINT RESOLUTION

Proposing an amendment to the Constitution extending the right of suffrage to women.

Resolved by the Senate and House of Representatives of the United States of America in Congress assembled (two-thirds of each House concurring therein), That the following article is proposed as an amendment to the Constitution, which shall be valid to all intents and purposes as part of the Constitution when ratified by the legislatures of three-fourths of the several States.

"ARTICLE ————.

"The right of citizens of the United States to vote shall not be denied or abridged by the United States or by any State on account of sex.

"Congress shall have power to enforce this article by appropriate legislation."

F. H. Gillett

Speaker of the House of Representatives.

Vice President of the United States and
President of the Senate.

Figure 1. The 19th Amendment to the United States Constitution. Archives.com

Call for Articles: Yearbook 2021

Women of Dutchess County, New York: Voices and Talents, Part II

Deadline: We are expecting submission of articles by **February 1, 2021**. We look forward with delight to reading your essays

The yearbook is planned to coordinate with the Dutchess County Historical Society's programming and continue the theme of the 2020 book by focusing on the lives and achievements of the women of our county. Topics can cover all of our history up to 50 years ago, our usual limit.

In 2021, as for the last several years, the yearbook will be divided into sections:

(1) The Forum section will focus on essays and stories about women of Dutchess County. Articles may include topics from the more abstract such as discussions of women within historical movements to quite concrete matters such as accounts of individual residents of the county.

(2) The Articles section will be devoted to essays on any worthwhile research regarding Dutchess County history.

Please submit your article to me in digital form as a Microsoft Word document. Articles for the Forum and Articles sections should be 2,000 to 4,000 words long. If possible, please submit at least one or two images with captions with each essay. Please check for copyright clearance. Send the images separately as jpegs (300 dpi or larger). Images may be black-and-white or color. Please send them with the draft, the figure captions indicated in the text (images are not an afterthought). Copyright will be shared between the Dutchess County Historical Society and the author. The author may re-issue the article in the year after it is published in the DCHS yearbook. DCHS asks that we be notified of any republication of your article.

Continued

For endnotes, please use *Chicago Manual of Style*. Examples of endnotes:

Franklin D. Roosevelt, 508th Press Conference, December 10, 1938, *Public Papers and Addresses of Franklin D. Roosevelt, 1938 Volume: The Continuing Struggle for Liberalism* (New York: Macmillan, 1941), 632.

Nancy V. Kelly, "Rhinebeck: Transition in 1799" in *The Hudson Valley Regional Review* Vol. 6, No. 2 (March 1989), 94.

If you have an idea for an article that you are considering, but are doubtful about, just write to me and I will be happy to discuss it.

— Candace Lewis, *Editor*

The Year in Review
Summer 2020

by Bill Jeffway
Executive Director

Writing mid-way through 2020, it seems the year will be remembered historically for the global pandemic, for the voices and demands relating to social justice and equality, and its tumultuous political arguments. Without diminishing the suffering caused by the pandemic and the corresponding "pause," as it was called in New York, the time at home allowed for some to reflect on small, day to day joys, *at hand*. And so, like life, the history we choose to remember so that future generations may do the same, includes the painful, the joyous, the large and small. "The things that we can see and touch… things that have happened on the spot…," were the words Louis Mumford used to describe local history as he spoke of its unique value and powers to DCHS members at Troutbeck in Amenia in 1927.

We continue to expand outreach through partnerships with the Poughkeepsie Public Library District, the FDR Presidential Library and Museum, the Barrett Art Center, and more recently, the Mid-Hudson Anti Slavery History Project. We have begun working with educators in public high schools to create trials of remote learning tools.

We have been putting a greater focus on sustaining conversations around important topics, such as:

Women. Under the umbrella concept of *2020 Focus: Women's Voices & Talents*, we profile women who had powerful political voices in the movement for women's equality on the 100th anniversary of women nationally achieving the right to vote. We examine the extraordinary talents of women of our county that range from the creative and artistic, to business and scientific.

The exhibition, *Rediscovering Caroline M. Clowes: An Important Nineteenth-Century American Painter* (see a sampling of her work in the Yearbook), is the main event, and will have many facets that range from a physical exhibition when safe to do so, to an ongoing online exhibition, and a printed catalogue of her work. Other Collections, gifts such as the work of 20th century painter Eunice Hatfield Smith (gift of Joan Smith) and usage rights secured from the Eastman Museum of Rochester for the

4-minute, 1917 silent training movie that features Poughkeepsie's Nina Mattern McCullough who died in the 1918 pandemic, are examples of other ways we are telling the story.

The 2020 Yearbook also will showcase this theme: *Women of Dutchess County, New York: Voices and Talents*. Woman suffrage will hold center stage with several articles on the topic. In addition, the life and work of Caroline M. Clowes, an important nineteenth century painter of animals will be examined along with the lives of other outstanding women in local history.

African Heritage and Black History. There is no doubt that much work remains to close the gap that remains in the telling of the full story of Black history in Dutchess County, a gap described by Lorraine Roberts and Lawrence Mamiya through the title of their 1987 DCHS Yearbook article, "Invisible People, Untold Stories."

The Poughkeepsie Equality Trail is a pilot educational online tool that shows how local people and places fit in the constellation of the national movement toward achieving the promise of equality. Building on the foundational collection given by the late Walter Patrice, DCHS is developing an online library that curates content related to the study of the experiences of those of African Heritage that draws from our collections and publications.

Veterans Voices. The exhibition launched in 2018, *Over Here: The Untold Stories of the Men, Women & Children of the World War 1917 to 1919*, travelled to virtually every city and town in the county, and now remains an online exhibition. Production on the educational and documentary version of that exhibition had to be put on hold due to the pandemic. The commitment to develop this series of on-demand videos remains firm and will start again when we are able to safely do so. We also had to pause our efforts to record the stories of living veterans that had been accelerated by a $10,000 grant from the Wilson Foundation.

Last fall, we enjoyed record attendance at the late 2019 Awards dinner. Congratulations again to: Myra Young Armstead, Ph.D., the Helen Wilkinson Reynolds Award for the pursuit of historical truth; Thomas S. Wermuth, Ph.D., the Helen Wilkinson Reynolds Award; Edward Downey, Esq., the Dutchess Award for community contributions; Adams Fairacre Farms, Business of Historic Distinction, Pat & Steve Adams accepting. (The Franklin D. Roosevelt Award for scholarship early in life, no award.)

The unique position of local history to educate calls on us to improve our work here. And we are pleased to announce that we have added an award that joins those just mentioned: the Eileen Mylod Hayden Award for excellence in teaching. Also, we are working with educators in public high schools, and at the college level, to create new support for teachers and professors.

A few of the significant supporters of our work are worth mentioning given either scale or long tenure of giving or both:the National Society Daughters of the American Revolution, the Lillian J. Cumming Fund of The Rhode Island Foundation, the Denise M. Lawler Fund at the Community Foundations of the Hudson Valley,the Wilson Foundation, Central Hudson, and Hudson Views and AAR Auctions.

Finally, the responsibility given to us to physically care for DCHS Collections for over a century is central to our mission. Recent acquisitions include:

From E. Stuart and Linda Hubbard we gratefully received additional paintings, drawings and items related to the artist mentioned earlier, Caroline Morgan Clowes. Combined with the Hart Hubbard Collection, DCHS holds a unique and comprehensive view into a family that mixed agriculture, education, and talent into a uniquely Dutchess County life.

In summary, we hope 2020 will prove to have been a year when DCHS, and Dutchess County, stepped up and adapted to adversity while protecting those things worth remembering. That includes the good and bad, the large and small. All this is done in the belief that we can strengthen the understanding, capacity and quality of life of future generations. Only time will tell.

Women working in munition factory

We are ready

to Work beside you,
Fight beside you and
Die beside you ——
Let us Vote beside you

VOTE FOR

WOMAN
SUFFRAGE

November 6th

FORUM

Campaigning for Woman Suffrage in Dutchess County

by Sandra Opdycke

The article in the *Poughkeepsie Daily Eagle* on Feb. 25, 1910, began like this:

> The Equal Suffrage League of Poughkeepsie was organized...
> on Monday evening, a constitution adopted and officers elected
> for the ensuing year...About thirty people were present. [1]

The founding of this League marked a turning-point in the story of woman suffrage in Dutchess County. As we will see, there had been several previous episodes of suffrage activity in the county, but the Equal Suffrage League was particularly significant, because of the scale of its efforts, and because of its participation in the climactic final years of women's campaign for the vote in New York State.

The Early Years

When did suffrage first become a live issue for Dutchess County women? The first recorded occasion was in 1874, at a meeting of the newly-organized local chapter of the Women's Christian Temperance Union. One of the members, Helen Loder, objected to the fact that the chapter's constitution required a focus on just one subject: the evils of alcohol. So Loder and 20 other women quit the WCTU and formed their own Prohibition and Equal Rights Society. "We struggled along . . . for about nine months," Loder recalled later, but "we were obliged to suspend operations for the want of means."[2] Within a decade, the WCTU would broaden its social goals and start supporting woman suffrage. But in 1874, Loder and her followers stood very much alone (Figure 1).

The issue of suffrage surfaced again in Dutchess County in 1880, when a new state law gave women the right to vote—and to run for office—in school elections. Immediately, public officials around the state began offering technical objections. Some insisted that the law, as written, applied only to rural districts. Others, including Poughkeepsie's City Attorney, maintained that the wording of their city charters prevented them from complying with the new law.[3] Then the state superintendent of schools weighed in, announcing (falsely) that the law applied only to women with extensive property holdings, and that if any other women voted, they could expect to spend six months in prison.[4] Faced with this chilly welcome, relatively few women in the state even tried to vote, and most of those who tried were turned away. In Poughkeepsie, one of the rejectees was Helen Loder, the former WCTU member, who by now had organized another suffrage society.[5] One of the few bright spots in Dutchess County that year was the town of Union Vale, where not only were women allowed to vote in the school election, but a young mother was elected Clerk of the local district.[6]

The next time suffrage was widely discussed in Dutchess County was in 1894, when New York State held one of its rare constitutional conventions. National suffrage leader Susan B. Anthony (who lived in Rochester) immediately launched a campaign to get votes for women written into the

Figure 1. Headquarters of the WCTU, 12 Cannon Street, Poughkeepsie, New York. N.d. Photograph. Collection of the Dutchess County Historical Society. By 1887, when the Poughkeepsie WCTU moved into this building (the former home of the Poughkeepsie Female Academy), the organization had become a strong supporter of woman suffrage, and a number of suffrage meetings were held here at WCTU headquarters.

new constitution. Part of her strategy was to deluge the constitutional convention with pro-suffrage petitions. Accordingly, she and her team sent out thousands of petition forms to suffragists all over the state.

In Dutchess County, the petition campaign began with a two-day conclave in Poughkeepsie that drew a crowd of about 100 people. Among the speakers was the indomitable Anthony—who, at age 74, managed to speak in every one of New York's 61 counties that spring. There does not seem to have been any formal suffrage group in Dutchess County at the time, but a Woman Suffrage Committee was organized and the women quickly started circulating the petitions around the county. Altogether, New York State suffragists gathered more than 500,000 signatures (compared to a paltry 15,000 collected by the anti-suffragists). But in the end, the delegates voted woman suffrage down, 98 to 58.[7]

So why did school suffrage for women face such resistance in 1880? And why did the campaign to include woman suffrage in the state constitution fail in 1894? The truth is that, although New York did not yet have much of a formal anti-suffrage *organization*, there was plenty of anti-suffrage *sentiment* around the state. Thousands of people—women as well as men—were convinced that for women to venture into the "male" sphere of politics—even school politics—would distract them from their God-given duties at home, and undermine their most precious qualities—their purity and their idealism.

It is true that by the 1890s, women were more active in public life than they had been a generation earlier; indeed, they were emerging as real leaders in the field of social reform. To the suffragists, this new public role further justified their claim to the vote. But many New Yorkers remained unconvinced. There were, for instance, liquor dealers and factory owners and machine politicians who feared that female voters would support reforms that would disrupt their customary way of doing things. There were working-class New Yorkers—male *and* female—who thought of suffrage as a rich woman's hobby. And there were conservatives and nativists who opposed any expansion of the electorate.

So the debate continued; the nineteenth century ended; and the women of New York State were still unenfranchised.

The National Campaign

These periodic efforts by New York State women to win the vote were part of a larger national campaign that had officially begun in 1848 in this very state, at the famous Seneca Falls convention on women's rights. By the late nineteenth century, many suffragists had concluded that their best long-term option would be to amend the U.S. Constitution, so that women could vote nationwide. But it seemed clear that Congress would not take their cause seriously until they had won a certain number of state victories. And getting suffrage adopted at the state level was no small task, because changing a state's voting qualifications meant amending that state's constitution. That generally required a two-thirds majority of each house of the legislature, and then a majority vote of the whole state electorate.

From the 1870s on, the suffragists mounted campaign after campaign in the states, but they were defeated again and again. In the early 1890s, four western states in a row did approve woman suffrage. It seemed like a breakthrough. But it would take 14 more years before the next state victory in 1910. And during those years, the suffragists lost their two great early leaders, Susan B. Anthony and Elizabeth Cady Stanton. Nevertheless, the movement steadily gained momentum—with stronger state organizations and rising membership numbers.

During these years, New York City emerged as a lively center of suffrage activity, featuring not one but two notable leaders. In 1909, Carrie Chapman Catt founded the Woman Suffrage Party, a highly disciplined group that was organized by electoral district—copying Tammany Hall—with levels of responsibility running right down to the smallest precinct. Around the same time, the Women's Political Union (WPU) was founded by Harriot Stanton Blatch, the daughter of Elizabeth Cady Stanton.[8] Having lived for many years in England, Blatch had learned a lot from the feisty British "suffragettes" about how to stir up public interest in their cause. Some of the Britishers' activities, such as blowing up telephone booths, were blatantly illegal. But Blatch's group focused on the suffragettes' more peaceable tactics—street-corner speaking, open-air rallies, and big parades—and these were soon picked up by other suffrage groups around the United States.

There is no evidence of organized suffrage activity in Dutchess County during the first years of the twentieth century. But thanks to regular coverage of the subject in Poughkeepsie's daily newspapers, local women were kept well aware of how the movement was progressing—the federal and state campaigns, the four western victories, the exploits of the British suffragettes, and the lively suffrage scene in New York City. And there must have been a community of eager readers, because when suffrage resurfaced in Dutchess County this time, it did so with remarkable vigor.

Launching the Equal Suffrage League

The first sign of new life was a well-attended evening of suffrage speeches held on December 1, 1909, in Poughkeepsie's most impressive auditorium, the Collingwood Opera House (now the Bardavon). The principal speaker was Mrs. Philip Snowden, a leading light of the British suffrage movement. And joining her on the platform were seven notable men and women from the community, including the Poughkeepsie mayor.[9]

One of the prime movers of the new wave of suffrage activity was Mary Swain Wagner, owner of the College Inn in Arlington. With some help from movement leaders in New York City, she and a group of local women (including several Vassar professors) organized the Collingwood meeting. At the same time, Wagner put out a call for people who might be interested in founding an Equal Suffrage League.[10] The list of names grew steadily longer, and in early January 1910, the *Poughkeepsie Evening Enterprise* observed, "The cause of equal suffrage is looking up in Poughkeepsie."[11] A few days later Swain and her colleagues staged a second meeting at the Collingwood, this one featuring another British suffragist, Ethel Arnold, as well as the dynamic young writer and activist Max Eastman.

Finally, on February 22, about 30 men and women gathered at Wagner's hotel, where they formally established the Poughkeepsie Equal Suffrage League. Laura Wylie (a Vassar professor who had been working with Wagner from the beginning) was elected president (Figure 7), while the job of Secretary-Treasurer went to Wagner herself. In addition, the members formed a kind of executive committee of 13 vice-presidents. There were seven women on the list, including the wife of the publisher of the *Poughkeepsie Daily Eagle*, the wife of the owner of the Nelson House, and two Vassar professors). The six men included a Vassar professor, the District Attorney, and a county judge.[12]

The makeup of the group at the founding meeting was reflective of the League's overall membership in the years to come. Although there were always some male members, women were in the majority, and they provided the leadership. In terms of background, most of the women were middle- or upper-middle-class—typically, the wives and daughters of local lawyers and doctors and businessmen. The group did have a few upper-class members, including Mrs. Gordon Norrie and Mrs. Richard Aldrich. But upper-class representation was small, since most women who belonged to the local elite (including Franklin D. Roosevelt's mother) opposed woman suffrage. The League also had relatively few working-class members.[13] During these years, some urban suffrage groups were building a more diverse membership, but Poughkeepsie's predominantly middle-class character was not unusual.

What did set thisLeague apart was its connection to Vassar College. For one thing, quite a few League members were Vassar graduates. Besides that, a number of Vassar's male professors joined the organization, and Vassar students often attended the League's public events. But Vassar's female professors played the largest role. These well-educated self-supporting single women became some of the League's most committed and influential members, providing two of the group's four presidents, 1910-1918.

Part of the reason that Vassar faculty and students chose to join a community-based suffrage organization like the League was because there was so little opportunity for suffrage activity at the college. James Taylor, a Baptist minister who served as Vassar's president through 1914, was convinced that opening the campus to suffrage "propaganda," as he called it, would disrupt the calm rational atmosphere that was needed to train young minds. (Taylor is especially remembered in suffrage history for the occasion in June 1908 when he told a student named Inez Milholland that she could not hold a suffrage meeting on campus. She then galvanized public attention by defiantly holding the meeting anyway, in a nearby graveyard.)[14]

Henry MacCracken, who succeeded Taylor in 1915, was personally a vocal supporter of woman suffrage, and he did permit the students to form a suffrage club. But, like Taylor, he firmly limited the number of suffrage lectures on campus, in part because many of the speakers the students wanted to invite were associated with a militant suffrage group called the Congressional Union, of which he disapproved. A number of Vassar alumnae belonged to the Union, including the now-graduated Inez Milholland. MacCracken was particularly reluctant to have Milholland on campus, both because of her radical views and because inviting her could be seen as a slap at his predecessor, President Taylor (Figure 2). But MacCracken's limits on suffrage meetings extended well beyond Milholland and the Congressional Union; overall during his tenure, he approved very few suffrage speakers, whatever their affiliation. Thus, from 1910 on, the Poughkeepsie Equal Suffrage League offered a welcome outlet for Vassar faculty and students who wanted to participate more actively in the suffrage movement than they could at the college.

Figure 2. Poster announcing an on-campus suffrage meeting at Vassar College, October 1915. Archives and Special Collections, Vassar College Library, Vassar College, Poughkeepsie, NY. In Oct. 1915, when Vassar's new president, Henry MacCracken, learned of this planned meeting, he immediately had it canceled. He told reporters he simply wanted to limit distractions during Vassar's 50th anniversary celebration. But it is clear that he also preferred not to provide a forum for Inez Millholland (Vassar '09) and her militant associates.

Doing Suffrage

Almost as soon as the Equal Suffrage League was founded, Harriot Blatch's group in New York City began urging the Poughkeepsie women to take up some of the newer publicity tactics that Blatch had brought back from England, including street-corner speaking and open-air rallies. Perhaps the League members were personally hesitant, or perhaps they thought those methods would not be effective in their rather conservative county. Whatever the reason, they instead devoted much of their energy to the more decorous task of sponsoring public lectures. They presented half a dozen each year, featuring a variety of speakers, including Vassar professors, suffrage activists from New York City, leaders from the national association, and visitors from western states that had adopted suffrage.

League members also began promoting suffrage in the rest of the county. They sponsored a tent at the Fair every year, offering daily speeches, as well as great quantities of literature and suffrage buttons. In addition, they began organizing suffrage groups in the outlying towns, so effectively that by 1915, there were at least nine of these groups—in Clinton Corners, Dover Plains, Hyde Park, Millbrook, New Hackensack, Pine Plains, Pleasant Valley, Red Hook, and Wappingers Falls. The Wappingers Falls group, led by a doctor's wife named Jessie Phinney, was particularly enterprising, offering a steady round of public events, including one of the first open-air rallies in the county. (Figure 3)

Figure 3. Jessie Woodward Phinney, ca. 1877.Photograph. Archives and Special Collections, Vassar College Library, Vassar College, Poughkeepsie, NY. Jessie Phinney, a Vassar College graduate, was the central figure of the lively Wappingers Equal Suffrage League. In addition, after the local suffrage movement was reorganized in 1913, she served as one of two district heads covering the whole county.

The Poughkeepsie papers were quite generous in their coverage of all these activities. Even Francis Platt at the *Poughkeepsie Daily Eagle*, who had no particular sympathy for woman suffrage, gave the local movement regular, quite balanced, attention. But there was one time, in late December 1912, when the local campaign was totally eclipsed. That was the week the "Suffrage Pilgrims"came to town. This small band of women, led by an enterprising New Yorker called "General" Rosalie Jones, was traveling *on foot* from New York City to Albany, to present a suffrage petition to the governor. Along the way, the Pilgrims spent five nights in Dutchess County— in Fishkill, Wappingers Falls, Poughkeepsie, Rhinebeck, and Red Hook. Despite the terrible winter weather, many local residents came out to greet them as they passed by. And at an overall factory in Wappingers Falls, the manager actually stopped the machinery so the Pilgrims could address the 500 women who worked there.He then assigned 20 of the women to accompany the Pilgrims on the next stage of their journey: the seven miles to Poughkeepsie. When the cavalcade reached the city, they found the streets decked with suffrage yellow banners, a crowd of admirers clamoring to meet them, and the mayor waiting at the Nelson House to give them the keys to the city. The next day the Pilgrims marched on to Rhinebeck, the following day to Red Hook, and then into Columbia County. The whole trip was breathlessly recorded by the local press, and it certainly conveyed an image of valiant suffragists in action.[15]

The Suffrage Pilgrims' visit was a reminder of the active campaign for the vote that was going on beyond Dutchess County's borders. By late 1912, five more states had approved suffrage, bringing the total to nine. But so far, not a single state east of the Mississippi had joined their ranks. What a coup it would be if New York, the largest state in the nation, could be added to the list! With that goal in mind, New York suffragists persistently lobbied the legislature to approve a suffrage amendment to the state constitution. Finally, in January 1913, the legislature said yes. But New York was one of many states that required amendments to be approved by *two* consecutive legislatures, so the bill would have to pass again in 1915 before going to the whole electorate.

Getting Serious

Despite the bridges still remaining to be crossed, the atmosphere among New York State suffragists changed once the legislature cast its critical-first vote in 1913. Organization became tighter, and the leaders of the state association worked more vigorously to bring the local societies into conformity with the overall state program. For example, the practice of organizing suffrage work by electoral district, first introduced by Carrie Chapman Catt in New York City, was now made nearly universal around the state. In Dutchess County this meant that the various local suffrage groups were gathered into two large districts, following the lines of the county's two Assembly Districts. One of the new districts was led by Jessie Phinney, head of the Wappingers Equal Suffrage League (Figure 3), and the other by Margaret Chanler Aldrich of Barrytown, a member of the Poughkeepsie League. Below the Assembly District level, there was a captain for each town, and in the larger towns, another level below that. The reorganization ruffled some local feathers, especially because it was clear that the state association was going to be playing a larger role in the county from now on. There was even some talk of disbanding the Poughkeepsie League. But the contention blew over, and the existing groups found a way to continue working within the new system.[16]

As part of the stepped-up campaign, a state organizer named Jessie Hardy Stubbs spent several weeks in Dutchess County during the summer of 1913, holding meetings and outdoor rallies in a dozen different towns. Stubbs, who had participated in the celebrated "suffrage hike" the previous December, brought such verve to her work that, according to a local reporter, "men who had never given suffrage a serious thought before, took a deep and sudden interest in the matter."[17] Stubbs even managed to persuade the cautious Poughkeepsie League members to sponsor their first (and only) grand suffrage parade.

The parade, which was held on July 4, 1913, was a spectacular affair, complete with row upon row of white-clad women walking four abreast, a float bearing the Statue of Liberty (the horses tried to run away but were stopped), another float on which the nine suffrage states were represented by nine beautiful girls, a contingent of 34 male supporters, a regimental band, yards of yellow ribbon, and a whirlwind of boys on bicycles. The procession started in Eastman Park, marched up Montgomery Street to South Hamilton, then over to Main Street, down Main to Market Street, and back to the park. Everyone agreed that one of the highlights of the day came when they reached the Old Ladies Home and found the ladies all out on the verandah, waving yellow flags. (Figure 4).[18]

Poughkeepsie never staged another demonstration quite as ambitious as that suffrage parade, but the event did reflect a change in the League's approach to its work. "From now on," said one of the members, "we are going to campaign in earnest."[19] One symbol of the change was the group's

Figure 4. Amenia Field Day, August 1913, Photograph. *Collier's Magazine*, 52, no. 1 (Sep. 20, 1913), p. 15. White-clad suffragists march at the Amenia Field Day in August 1913, looking very much the way they must have looked just a few weeks earlier at the grand suffrage parade in Poughkeepsie.

decision to move its Poughkeepsie headquarters to a more accessible location—on Market Street—and to keep it open more hours every day. And while the League continued to present public lectures from time to time, most of its activities from 1913 on were designed to reach a wider circle of county residents—including people who would never bother to attend a suffrage lecture, and those who might feel uncomfortable in grand venues like the Collingwood Opera House.

The secret to reaching a broader audience was, of course, to go where the people were. Accordingly, the League changed its policy and began holding regular open-air rallies—in towns around the county and frequently at the corner of Main and Market Street in Poughkeepsie. At the same time, the members began doing more speaking to community groups, addressing everyone from the Socialists to the Knights of Columbus, as well as firemen, teachers, church ladies, factory workers, and ten different Mothers' Clubs. The League also made its first outreach to Poughkeepsie's African-American community, with a visit to the local AME Zion church.

Another way to reach the unconvinced was with a party, and the suffragists embraced this tactic as well. When the county Grange association gathered in Poughkeepsie for its annual convention, the League treated the entire membership to lunch at the Nelson House. Meanwhile, suffrage societies in the outlying towns produced a succession of teas, oyster suppers, dances, and bridge parties. The suffrage message was always in the air at these events, but presumably it went down easier when combined with food and festivity.

In early 1915, the state legislature approved the suffrage amendment for the second time, thus clearing the way for it to go on the ballot in November. With the final goal in sight, the Dutchess County suffragists redoubled their efforts. The local anti-suffragists also picked up their pace. The antis had not been particularly active in the past, probably because there had seemed to be little danger of the state's adopting woman suffrage. But in 1915, with the amendment actually on the ballot, the anti-suffragists began holding more public meetings, writing more letters to the newspapers, and in September they even set up their own booth at the County Fair.

When Election Day finally arrived, it began badly for the suffragists. There in the morning paper was a long editorial by the publisher, Francis Platt, opposing the amendment. Although everyone knew that Platt did not favor suffrage, he had usually been fairly restrained in his comments, perhaps because his mother, wife, and daughter were all dedicated suf-fragists. But now he made his position clear. He acknowledged that his father (the paper's previous publisher) had supported suffrage, but Platt suggested that if his father were alive today, he would surely change his mind. "The movement for suffrage," wrote Platt, "has been sweeping eastward too fast to be entirely sane and wholesome." He claimed that where suffrage had been adopted, it had produced "radical and half-baked experiments in government." He seriously questioned whether suffrage was right for New York. More fundamentally, he questioned whether the mass of New York's "normal, refined, home-loving women" even wanted to vote.[20]

Did other New Yorkers share Platt's doubts about suffrage? It turned out they did. When the election results were tallied, they showed that the amendment had been defeated in 56 out of the state's 61 counties. And among those rejecting counties was Dutchess, where the amendment won only 40% of the vote. As for Poughkeepsie, suffrage was defeated there in every single ward.[21]

It says something about the spirit of the New York State suffragists that, within days of their defeat, they started raising money for the next campaign. As part of the reorganization that followed, the state association changed its name to the one Carrie Chapman Catt had used in New York City—the Woman Suffrage Party. The Poughkeepsie League followed suit, becoming the Poughkeepsie Suffrage Party. And so, with a new name but the same goal, the women resumed their campaigning, while suffragists in Albany started lobbying for another vote in 1917.

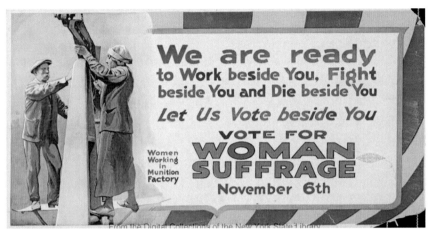

Figure 5. "We are ready to work beside you, Fight beside you and Die beside you—VOTE FOR WOMAN SUFFRAGE November 6th." This 1917 billboard reminds passers-by of the upcoming suffrage referendum, while stressing the connection between New York women's ongoing contribution to the war effort and their worthiness for the vote. Billboard promoting woman suffrage, 1917. Collections of New York State Library, Manuscripts and Collections, Albany NY, SC23360, USGEN-94.

The Last Push

In early January 1917, the Legislature approved sending the suffrage amendment to the voters again that November. The Dutchess County women carried on with their lectures and parties and rallies, adding one new wrinkle: their messages now began appearing on the screen at the movies while the projectionist was changing reels. In addition, League members intensified their outreach to working-class voters, especially in Poughkeepsie's 1st Ward (the principal immigrant neighborhood), where the amendment had done particularly badly in 1915.

Would these efforts have been enough to carry the vote in November 1917? We will never know. Because in April 1917 came the ultimate game-changer: the United States entered World War I. American suffragists were immediately faced with a dilemma. Should they continue to campaign for their own cause, or should they switch over to working for the war effort? Carrie Chapman Catt, now president of the national suffrage association, had a decisive answer: "We must do both!"[22]

And that was the line the suffragists followed in Dutchess County. Between April and November 1917, they continued to organize public lectures and parties and rallies, especially as Election Day drew closer. But much of their attention now went to the war effort. At the time, the government was urging American women to help sustain the Allies by growing and preserving more food. The Dutchess County suffragists zeroed in on canning as their special project. They offered classes in canning; they helped coordinate canning activities around the county; and they continually solicited more volunteers. Their work received glowing coverage in the local papers, and of course every time the papers publicized the work, they also publicized the suffragists' patriotic involvement in it (Figure 5).

The more praise the suffragists received for their war efforts, the more irritated the county's anti-suffragists became. The local leader, Mrs. A. C. Rust, sent a flurry of letters to the local papers, insisting that the suffragists' motives were purely political. The antis also announced several new war-work projects of their own.[24] But the suffragists' favorable publicity just kept building. In September, they scored another hit, when the suffrage societies in Amenia, Staatsburg, Beacon, Millbrook, Pawling, and Wingdale together produced enough pies to feed all 800 members of the local Home Defense unit. "The men gave cheer after cheer for the bounty of the Suffrage Party," reported the *Eagle-News*, "and declared that such good cooks would make good voters."[25]

And so Election Day 1917 arrived. This time, the vote-count produced both good news and bad news. The good news was that, after losing Poughkeepsie in 1915, this time the suffragists had eked out a narrow victory (50.3%, up from 37% in 1915). This made Poughkeepsie one of the very few Hudson River cities, from Yonkers all the way to Saratoga, that had now passed the amendment. Almost every ward in the city had a higher pro-suffrage vote than in 1915, and among the immigrant voters of the 1st Ward, the percentage of "yes" votes had soared from 36% to 73%. The bad news was that the victory in Poughkeepsie had not been enough to carry Dutchess County. The amendment got 47% of the vote county-wide, and although that was significantly better than 1915, it was not enough to win[28] (Figure 6).

Figure 6. Dutchess County Results: 1917 Woman Suffrage Referendum, New York State

Percent in favor:

Amenia	49	Pawling	60
Beacon	50	Pine Plains	54
Beekman	54	Pleasant Valley	41
Clinton	37	Poughkeepsie (City)	50
Dover	61	Poughkeepsie (Town)	45
E. Fishkill	49	Red Hook	43
Fishkill	54	Rhinebeck	40
Hyde Park	41	Stanford	53
LaGrange	49	Union Vale	58
Northeast	48	Wappingers	39
		Washington	47

County-wide: 47%

Source: Dutchess County Supervisors, *Annual Report: 1917*

But the best news was that a strong pro-suffrage tide in New York City had outweighed losses upstate and carried the amendment to victory state-wide by a margin of 100,000.[30] Sixty-nine years after the Seneca Falls convention, New York State women had won the right to vote.

Dutchess County suffragists exulted in the outcome. They realized that they owed their thanks for the final result to the men of other counties, not their own. But they could still take pleasure in the Poughkeepsie victory, as well as in the fact that in the two years since 1915, the pro-suffrage vote in the county had risen from 40% to 47%. And whatever the path, they now had the vote. So we can understand the joyous applause that erupted at a public meeting a few days after the election, when the principal speaker began by welcoming the ladies in the audience with these words: "Fellow citizens..."[31]

The Rest of the Story

Experience had shown that, once a state adopted suffrage, its representatives in Congress were more likely to support the federal suffrage amendment too. You could see that process at work when the amendment came to a vote in the U.S. House of Representatives in January 1918, just two months after New York State approved woman suffrage. A few years earlier, only nine of New York's 43 House members had voted for the federal amendment. In 1918, that number rose to 33.[32] (Among the New Yorkers who voted yes that day was Edmund Platt of Poughkeepsie—co-owner with his brother Francis of the *Poughkeepsie Eagle-News*, and a man who had always opposed woman suffrage in the past.)[33]

And so it happened that on January 10, 1918, with a significant boost from the New York delegation,the suffrage amendment won exactly the number of votes needed to pass the House. The suffragists would spend many more months getting it through the Senate, and then through 36 state legislatures, until finally, in August, 1920, it entered the Constitution as the 19th Amendment. But relatively few Dutchess County suffragists participated in that effort. From the beginning, most of them had concentrated

Figure 7. 112 Market Street, Poughkeepsie, NY, n.d. Photograph. Archives and Special Collections, Vassar College Library, Vassar College, Poughkeepsie, NY. This house, facing Soldiers' Fountain on Market Street in Poughkeepsie, was the home of Vassar professor Laura Wylie, president of both the Poughkeepsie Equal Suffrage League and the Women's City and County Club. When Wylie died, she left her house to the WCCC. The building later housed the Hudson River Clearwater Sloop, Inc.

on the local campaign, and when that fight was won, they turned their attention to the next local challenge: establishing themselves as voters and citizens in their own community.

The first step came on January 25, 1918, when the Poughkeepsie Suffrage Party transformed itself into the Women's City Club (renamed the Women's City and County Club in 1919). This was the new club's mission: "To enlist women in the cause of good government." The members chose as their leader Laura Wylie, who had been their first president and had recently accepted the League presidency again. The WCCC developed into a lively center of women's civic activity, especially in its first decade, when it attracted as many as 500 members and carried on an ambitious program of social investigation and public-interest lobbying. Often working in cooperation with the newly-formed League of Women Voters, the WCCC continued into the 1960s[34] (Figure 7). As a sequel to the suffrage movement, the club represented another significant chapter in the long story of Dutchess County women's aspirations and achievements—a story that began generations ago, that shone brilliantly during the suffrage years, and that continues today.

---

[1]   *Poughkeepsie Daily Eagle* (Feb. 25, 1910), p.7. I would like to express my appreciation to the many people who helped me gather information for this essay, including Dean Rogers, Special Collections Assistant, Vassar College Library; Beth Devine, President, and Sandra Vacchio, Treasurer & Archives, Wappingers Historical Society; Kira Thompson, Local History Librarian, Poughkeepsie Public Library District; and most especially Bill Jeffway, Executive Director, Dutchess County Historical Society. I would also like to thank Stacey Reid for her invaluable assistance during this time.

[2]   Helen Loder, "Poughkeepsie Letter: A Leaf from the Experience of a Suffragist," *Ballot Box* 1 no. 8 (Nov. 1876).

[3]   *Poughkeepsie Daily Eagle* (Nov. 16, 1880), p.2.

[4]   Sue Boland, "The Power of Women: Matilda Joslyn Gage and the New York Women's Vote of 1880," New York History 100, no. 1 (Summer 2019), 44; Bill Jeffway, "The Long and Winding Road: The Local Path to 1920 Women's Right to Vote" (Dutchess County Historical Society), at https://dchsny. org/1920localpath. [Rural districts did have modest tax-paying requirements, but they did not apply to the parents of school-children, and they certainly did not involve prison terms. Elizabeth Cady Stanton *et al.*, *History of Woman Suffrage*, v. 3, ch. 37, pp.423-425, at http://gutenberg.org.]

[5] *Poughkeepsie Daily Eagle* (Sept. 2, 1880), p.3; "Helen M. Loder, on the School Question," *National Citizen & Ballot Box* (Jan. 1881); *Poughkeepsie Daily Eagle* (Oct. 30, 1893), p.6.

[6] *New York Times* (Oct. 17, 1880), p.7. Loder would keep trying to vote in school elections for years, but she never prevailed.

[7] "New York State Suffrage Campaign: 1893-1894," at https://rrlc.org/winningthevote.nys-suffrage-1893; *Poughkeepsie Daily Eagle* (Mar. 7, 1894), p.8, and (Mar. 18, 1894), p.6. The proposed new state constitution was rejected by New York State voters, so the previous constitution remained in place.

[8] Initially called the League of Self-Supporting Women, the group changed its name to Women's Political Union in 1910.

[9] *Poughkeepsie Evening Enterprise* (Dec. 2, 1909), p.6.

[10] *Poughkeepsie Evening Enterprise* (Jan. 7, 1910), p.1, and (Jan. 10, 1910), p.1; *Poughkeepsie Daily Eagle* (Jan. 11, 1910), p.5; and *Poughkeepsie Eagle-News* (Feb. 21, 1920), p.6.

[11] *Poughkeepsie Evening Enterprise* (Jan. 10, 1910), p.1.

[12] *Poughkeepsie Evening Enterprise* (Feb. 22, 1910), p. 8; *Poughkeepsie Daily Eagle* (Feb. 25, 1910), p.7.

[13] David Kevin McDonald, "Organizing Womanhood: Women's Culture & the Politics of Woman Suffrage in New York State, 1865-1917" (Ph.D. diss., SUNY at Stony Brook, 1987), pp. 244-257.

[14] Candace J. Lewis, "Inez: Icon of a Movement," *Dutchess County Historical Society 2017 Yearbook* 96 (Poughkeepsie NY: Dutchess County Historical Society, 2017), p.85. For more on suffrage at Vassar, see: Eva C. Boice, "Woman Suffrage, Vassar College, and Laura Johnson Wylie," *Hudson River Valley Review* 20 (Spring 2004), pp.39-42; McDonald, "Organizing Womanhood," pp.241-243; Dale Mezzacappa, "*Vassar College* and the Suffrage Movement," *Vassar Quarterly* 69, no. 3 (Mar. 1, 1973); pp.2-9; "The Suffrage Movement at Vassar," *Vassar Encyclopedia*, at http://vcencyclopedia.vassar.edu/interviews-reflections/the-suffrage-movement.html.

[15] Jane Mathews Swersey, "General Rosalie Jones and the 'Votes for Women' March to Albany: Creating a New Political Activism," *Hudson River Valley Review* 35, no. 2 (Spring 2019), pp.36-42; Tiffany Lewis, "Mediating Political Mobility as Stunt-Girl Entertainment: Newspaper Coverage of New York's Suffrage Hike to Albany," *American Journalism* 36, no. 1 (2019), pp.114-16.

[16] *Poughkeepsie Evening Enterprise* (Sept. 24, 1913), p.10; (Oct. 7, 1913), p.2; and (Oct. 29, 1913), p.2.

[17] *Poughkeepsie Evening Enterprise* (June 2, 1913), p.10.

[18] *Poughkeepsie Daily Eagle* (July 8, 1913), p.3.

[19] *Poughkeepsie Evening Enterprise* (Dec. 2, 1913), p.8.

[20] *Poughkeepsie Eagle-News* (Nov. 2, 1915), p.4. In April 1915, the *Poughkeepsie Daily Eagle* merged with the *Poughkeepsie News-Telegraph*, forming the *Poughkeepsie Eagle-News*.

[21] Rusty C. Tobin, "Who Voted for Woman Suffrage: 1915 & 1917 New York State Suffrage Referenda," *New York History* 98, no. 3-4 (Summer/Fall 2017), p.438; *Poughkeepsie Eagle-News* (Nov. 5, 1915), p.2. Calculations by the author.

[22] Maud Wood Park, *Front Door Lobby* (Boston MA: Beacon Press, 1960), p.62.

[23] *Poughkeepsie Evening Enterprise* (Apr. 27, 1917), p.10; (May 26, 1917), p.1; and (Aug. 3, 1917), p.11.

[24] See, for instance, *Poughkeepsie Eagle-News* (Apr. 27, 1917), p.6; and (Sept. 18, 1917), p.3. Also *Poughkeepsie Evening Enterprise* (Sept. 14, 1917), p.10.

[25] *Poughkeepsie Eagle-News* (Sept. 21, 1917), p.4.

[26] McDonald, "Organizing Womanhood," p.237.

[27] *Poughkeepsie Eagle-News* (Nov. 5, 1915), p.2, and (Nov. 7, 1917), 5. Calculations by author.

[28] Dutchess County Board of Supervisors, *Annual Report*: 1917 (Poughkeepsie NY: Board of Supervisors, 1917), p.508.

[29] Ibid., pp.506-508.Note: One adjustment has been made, where the Supervisors' Report made a clerical error in the vote count for the 7th Ward, 2nd District. Correct data come from the *Poughkeepsie Eagle-News* (Nov. 7, 1917), p.5, confirmed by *Poughkeepsie Evening Star* (Nov. 5, 1917), p.1, and Poughkeepsie *Sunday Courier* (Nov. 11, 1917), p.6. Calculations by the author.

[30] Tobin, "Who Voted for Woman Suffrage," p.423.

[31] *Poughkeepsie Eagle-News* (Nov. 10, 1917), p.5.

[32] Park, *Front Door Lobby*, pp.154-45.

[33] Mezzacappa, "Vassar College and the Suffrage Movement," p.9.

[34] Harvey Flad, *Main Street to Main Frames: Landscape and Social Change in Poughkeepsie* (Albany NY: SUNY Press, 2009), pp.111-112; Boice, "Woman Suffrage, Vassar College, and Laura Johnson Wylie," pp.43-44.

Recovering the Paintings and Legacy of a Great American Artist: Caroline Morgan Clowes (1838-1904)

by Bill Jeffway

Through the extraordinary Caroline Morgan Clowes Collection, with its dozens of paintings, hundreds of sketches, photographs, and daguerreotypes, and thousands of pages from letters, diaries, event programs, and newspaper clippings, we are afforded a rare and personal insight into a woman born 182 years ago. In addition to the beauty and accomplishment reflected in Clowes' work, we find a personal story of a woman's persistence in a male-dominated field that resonates today.

Figure 1. Caroline M. Clowes, Buckskin, n.d. Oil on board. The Dutchess County Historical Society, The Caroline M. Clowes Collection, Gift of Linda and E. Stuart Hubbard, 2019. Buckskin was the horse that Caroline's cousin Ambrose Hart brought back from the South upon his return from the Civil War. The date of this work, therefore, would probably fall early in Miss Clowes' career, c. 1865-70. This, like all the Clowes works pictured in this article, come from the family home, "Heartsease" in La Grange, where they were created and where they were stored until donation to the Dutchess County Historical Society. Of the large number of works from this location—including paintings, drawings, diaries, and letters—a small proportion were dated or signed.

The general public will again be introduced to the work and life of one of America's greatest nineteenth-century painters, a specialist in animals and landscape. A display of Caroline M. Clowes' paintings and drawings, planned for exhibit at the Barrett House in Poughkeepsie, New York in September 2020 (baring any issues related to the pandemic, unknown as we go to press), will be available online. The exhibit, "Caroline Morgan Clowes (1838-1904): An Important Nineteenth-Century American Animal Painter," will be drawn from a generous gift of paintings, drawings, and archives (The Caroline Morgan Clowes Collection, from Linda and E. Stuart Hubbard to the Dutchess County Historical Society in 2019). It will present Miss Clowes' story again for the first time in over one hundred years. During her life, Miss Clowes became an accomplished painter, working in the wake of the Hudson River School artists, creating a reputation for herself as a virtuoso painter of animals and landscapes (Figures 1 and 2). She lived and worked at a large family home, "Heartsease," in LaGrange, here in Dutchess County. Miss Clowes was also closely associated with a number of members of the new institution of education for women, Vassar College—among them: Frederick Rondel, a painter connected to college founder Matthew Vassar and Henry Van Ingen, head of the Art Department. Even though she spent her entire life in Dutchess County, she exhibited widely—and with the finest male painters of her day.

In her purse, with some coins, Caroline carried a newspaper clipping.[1] It is a letter to the editor from January 22, 1881. The letter is written by a woman who pushed back hard on a recent talk entitled "A Model Wife," given by a man who argued that a woman's role was to be submissive to her husband. Underlined in pencil, presumably by Caroline, is the sentence reading, "if we've learned anything this century, it is that a woman deserves the place that she creates." In a letter to her sister while still a teenager, Caroline declared she was wedded to her easel.[2] It seems she had decided early on that a man would not be directing her future.

Childhood of Caroline M. Clowes

Caroline was two years old and living in Neversink Bridge, Sullivan County, when her mother died Christmas Eve, 1840.[3] Her infant sister died a few months later. Caroline and her sister Lydia, who was two years older, were raised by their single-parent father until Caroline was 13. William J. Clowes was trying to make a living managing lands in Orange and Sullivan County he had obtained through tenuous rights based on his ancestor Gerhardus Clowes, who was Orange County Clerk in the 1720s and a land conveyor. He sarcastically referred to land near the Minisink Patent as the

Figure 2. Caroline M. Clowes, Autumn Landscape, n.d. Oil on board. The Dutchess County Historical Society, The Caroline M. Clowes Collection, Gift of Linda and E. Stuart Hubbard, 2019.

"Moneysink Patent."[4] Equally unsuccessful financially, having invested in a printing press and publishing monographs on the topic,[5] he promoted a theory that numeric patterns in the Bible needed to be understood as they could bridge the gap between Biblical claims and scientific discovery. While he described God as the inventor and source of the "Apographean Numbers," he described himself, and offered himself as an "agent to the world" for their interpretation.[6]

Young Caroline Moves to Heartsease in LaGrange

In 1851, at age 13, Caroline was moved to the LaGrange home of her late mother's younger brother, Benjamin Hall Hart and his wife, Elizabeth (nee Nichols), whom she called "Aunt Elizabeth." Benjamin and Elizabeth Hart had seven children of their own. Lydia was relocated to Virginia, to the family of her late mother's older brother, William Henry Hart. William's daughter Elizabeth raised Lydia in Virginia with her husband, the Rev. Reuben Lindsay Coleman.

At this time, Dutchess County and Poughkeepsie were progressive when it came to the education of "young ladies." Among the more prominent co-educational schools were the Methodist Amenia Seminary and the Quaker Nine Partners Boarding School. Lucretia Coffin Mott, one of the five organizers of the 1848 Seneca Falls Convention on women's rights, was both a student and a teacher at the Nine Partners School. Poughkeepsie had four girls' schools at the time[7], Cook's Collegiate Institute, Miss Lydia Booth's Female Seminary, Cottage Hill, and the Poughkeepsie Female Academy that Caroline attended. Poughkeepsie was already referred to as the "City of Schools" when Matthew Vassar opened the "Vassar Female College" in 1865.

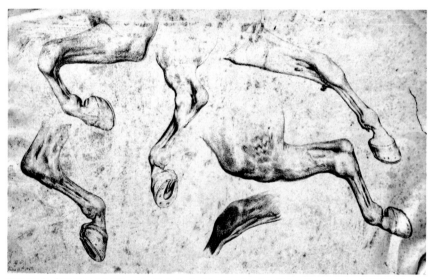

Figure 3. Caroline M. Clowes, Drawing of horses' legs. Signed and dated: "CMC June 12th 1862." Pencil sketch. The Dutchess County Historical Society, The Caroline M. Clowes Collection, Gift of Linda and E. Stuart Hubbard, 2019.

Benjamin and Elizabeth Hart raised Caroline with seven of their own children at the LaGrange farm they called "Heartsease." Home to what grew into an international apple business over three generations, they created a culture that was ambitious in business, art, and society, but compassionate, humble, and nurturing. Also living at Heartsease was Elizabeth Hart's mother, Elizabeth (1780-1858) and her sister, Louisa Adelia Nichols (1818-1892), whom Caroline called "Miss Nichols."[8] Miss Nichols had a vital role in the education of her young relative. A skilled artist herself, Louisa Nichols gave Caroline a gift of five drawing books for Christmas of 1851. Caroline wrote to her sister of the gift, "I hope I shall soon learn to draw well..."[9]

May 2, 1853, when Caroline was 15, her sister Lydia mentioned the "improvement in [Caroline's] drawing." In the same letter, Caroline's "Aunt Lizzie" wrote noting that Caroline's mother was talented in painting or drawing, "I hope you will equal your dear mother in the beautiful art of which you are so fond..."[10]

In 1854, Caroline's drawings were featured in an unnamed exhibition (Figure 3).[11] In 1856, at the end of what may have been a brief hiatus, Lydia wrote, "I am glad you are again hoping to take up your drawing and painting..."[12] In 1859, Lydia described Caroline as walking on school days from Heartsease to Poughkeepsie Female Academy on Cannon Street, a 45-minute walk each way. She mentions Caroline's taking art and drawing lessons from "Miss Dudgeon." In April of 1859, Caroline went to New York City with pictures. There is specific reference to "oils" and "larger pieces" in what may have been the first city trip with this purpose.

Two Important Men: Frederick Rondel and Henry Van Ingen

If the majority of instruction and support of the 1850s came from her aunt's sister, Miss Nichols, and Miss Dudgeon at the Poughkeepsie Female Academy, the 1860s saw the emergence of two men she would engage with for the rest of their lives: the French-born Frederick Rondel and Dutch-born Henry Van Ingen.

Rondel was a tutor, an advocate creating connections and recommendations for the exhibition and sale of her work, and even an artistic collaborator on individual works.[13]

Rondel arrived in the U.S. in October of 1856. He was engaged with New York City's National Academy of Design by 1861, an organization that would become important for Caroline. He settled in Poughkeepsie by January of 1862, offering to teach young ladies at first in his home studio at Mansion Square and Clinton Street, then on Main Street, Poughkeepsie. At the same time he taught at Cottage Hill and Poughkeepsie Female Academy, mentioned earlier. Between 1862 and 1867, he was retained by Matthew Vassar to create paintings of the Vassar ancestral home in England, and the first and then current Vassar residential homes in Poughkeepsie. During this period, he painted or sketched local scenes along the Hudson River and into the Adirondacks. Within Dutchess County, his works included views from Tivoli, Dover, Lake Sepasco in Rhinebeck, and the town of Milan's Rock City Mill. He moved to New Rochelle in 1871,

Figure 4. Caroline M. Clowes, Hens and chicks, n.d. Unsigned. Oil on board. The Dutchess County Historical Society, The Caroline M. Clowes Collection, Gift of Linda and E. Stuart Hubbard, 2019.

but kept in touch with Caroline Clowes for what appears to have been the rest of his life. In 1889, three years before his death, she wrote to Rondel seeking his sketching for a background of a "buff heifer."[14]

Henry Van Ingen emigrated to the U.S. in the 1850s. He was recruited by Matthew Vassar to create and lead Vassar College's Art School, which was eventually brought into the College as a department, and to establish an art museum. Van Ingen was highly regarded and served in that role until his death in 1898. He was the last of the original professors to pass away.

Van Ingen was known for leading students out of the classroom to sketch nature. Among the likely destinations was Heartsease, where Caroline had her studio. In one note to her he writes, "I promised some young ladies, (my most advanced pupils) to introduce them to Miss Clowes the artist, when they would have an opportunity to see some of her work, also." In 1878, he ensured that the Art Museum acquired a painting of hers, called "Contentment;" it shows a white calf resting comfortably in the shade of a tree. In one of the best descriptions of the magic Clowes achieves in depicting animals, the "Vassar Miscellany" applauds what may sound contradictory, "...*those transparently solid flesh tints!*"[16]

The Style of Caroline M. Clowes

At a time when interest in the Hudson River School, a uniquely American School, was declining in favor of European styles and subjects, Caroline Clowes embraced the concept of local Hudson Valley landscape painting, making it unique by focusing, close up, on animals. As a bonus to those interested specifically in the history of Dutchess County, we are delighted that she focused on the local farmscapes around her. Subjects include her cousin Ambrose's horse, "Buckskin" brought back from the South after the Civil War. She depicted the prized, "fattened steer" of her neighbor, George Ayrault. She painted, "Two cows near Wappinger Creek" in 1882 as a wedding present to her cousin (Figure 5), Louisa A. Hart. One painting is described as "near the Degarmo farm."

Figure 5. Caroline M. Clowes, *Two Cows at Wappingers Creek*, titled by the artist, signed "C.M. Clowes, 1882." The Dutchess County Historical Society, The Caroline M. Clowes Collection, Gift of Linda and E. Stuart Hubbard, 2019.

Figure 6. Exhibition Pass for 1876 Centennial Exhibition in Philadelphia. Pass issued to Caroline M. Clowes with her image reproduced from a portrait photograph.

Figure 7. Gallery C at 1876 Centennial Exhibition in Philadelphia. Stereograph, Centennial Photographic Company, 1876 The Free Libribrary of Philadelphia with annotations and edited to show location of Clowes painting, *Cattle at the Brook*.

The Philadelphia 1876 Centennial Exhibition

Between May and November, 1876, more than 10 million people attended the Centennial International Exhibition in Philadelphia[17], marking the 100th anniversary of the birth of the United States. Featuring all aspects of the best of America, art was displayed prominently. In a letter to Caroline in advance of the Exhibition, Poughkeepsie's Helen Hooker Stuyvesant Sanford wrote that she was appointed to manage matters related to local contributions. Reflecting, perhaps, what Caroline's achievements meant to many women at the time, she wrote, "As a woman I am so proud of your beautiful animals that I wish so much to have all the world see what a woman can do. I write to know if you will not send on a picture for the women's department at Philadelphia?"[18]

Figure 8. Caroline M. Clowes, Sheep in the Forest, n.d. Unsigned. The Dutchess County Historical Society, The Caroline M. Clowes Collection, Gift of Linda and E. Stuart Hubbard, 2019.

What Mrs. Stanford did not know, was that plans were already well under way to feature "Cattle at the Brook," not in the women's department, but in the main gallery. And within the main gallery, the painting would be featured in the most coveted gallery, "Gallery C," among the greats, America's best known male painters like Bierstadt, Kensett and Cole.[19] While some complained that Caroline's painting was "skied" (hung too high, in the fashion of the time of having paintings run nearly floor-to-ceiling), she must have taken some satisfaction in the achievement of what had been only a dream and a set of drawing books on Christmas Day at Heartsease 25 years earlier.

Conclusion

We don't know what the trajectory of Caroline's professional and personal life would have been had she relocated elsewhere. But in Dutchess County, the 13-year old Caroline found progressive thinking toward the education of women, a family with skilled women artists, encouragement of self-discovery and realization from the family's men and women within the four walls and farm affectionately called Heartsease, a vibrant intellectual community at the new Vassar College, and plenty of sheep, chickens, cows, horses, and farmscapes and landscapes to inspire her.

Figure 9. Caroline M. Clowes, Evensong titled by the artist, n.d. (c. 1880s. Understood to be one of Miss Clowes' last paintings.) Oil painting. The Dutchess County Historical Society, The Caroline M. Clowes Collection, Gift of Linda and E. Stuart Hubbard, 2019.

---

[1] Textual record. The Hart Hubbard Collection, Dutchess County Historical Society, Poughkeepsie, NY.

[2] Lydia M. Clowes' letter to Caroline M Clowes (May 3, 1859), Textual record, Hart Hubbard Collection, Dutchess County Historical Society, Poughkeepsie, NY.

[3] Elizabeth H. Clowes' letters to Lydia M. Clowes, Caroline M. Clowes, and Ellen L. Clowes" (Dec. 21, 1840), Textual records, Hart Hubbard Collection, Dutchess County Historical Society, Poughkeepsie, NY.

[4] Textual record, Hart Hubbard Collection, Dutchess County Historical Society, Poughkeepsie, NY

[5] Lydia M. Clowes' letter to Caroline M Clowes (Dec. 3, 1854), Textual record, Hart Hubbard Collection, Dutchess County Historical Society, Poughkeepsie, NY.

[6] Wm. J. Clowes, "'Apographean Numbers,' Letter to the Editor," *The Port Jervis Evening Gazette* (Oct. 17, 1876).

[7] Edmund Platt, *History of Poughkeepsie From the Earliest Settlements 1683 to 1905* (Poughkeepsie: Platt & Platt, 1905), pp. 125, 254.

[8] "La Grange, Dutchess, New York," *1860 US Federal Census*, p. 698.

[9] Caroline M. Clowes' letter to Lydia M. Clowes (Jan. 8, 1852), Textual record, Hart Hubbard Collection, Dutchess County Historical Society, Poughkeepsie, NY.

[10] Lydia M. Clowes and Elizabeth H. Coleman's letter to Caroline M. Clowes (May 2, 1853), Textual record, Hart Hubbard Collection, Dutchess County Historical Society, Poughkeepsie, NY.

[11] Lydia M. Clowes' letter to Caroline M. Clowes (April 2, 1854), Textual record, Hart Hubbard Collection, Dutchess County Historical Society, Poughkeepsie, NY.

[12] Lydia M. Clowes' letter to Caroline M. Clowes" (April 17, 1856), Textual record, Hart Hubbard Collection, Dutchess County Historical Society, Poughkeepsie, NY.

[13] Rondel letters.

[14] Textual record. The Hart Hubbard Collection, Dutchess County Historical Society, Poughkeepsie, NY.

[15] HenryVan Ingen Biographical File, Special Collections, Vassar College Library, Poughkeepsie, NY.

[16] *Vassar Miscellany* (November 1878).

[17] Linda P. Gross and Theresa R. Snyder, *Philadelphia's 1876 Centennial Exhibition* (Charleston, SC: Arcadia Publishing, 2005), pp. 7-8.

[18] Helen Sanford's letter to Caroline M. Clowes (May 10, 1876), Textual record, Hart Hubbard Collection, Dutchess County Historical Society, Poughkeepsie, NY.

[19] United States Centennial Commission, *International Exhibition 1876 Official Catalogue*, (Philadelphia, Pennsylvania: J.R. Nagle and Co, 1876).

The League of Women Voters in Dutchess County: Its Origin and Accomplishments

by Eleanor Rubin Charwat

From its founding in 1925 to its merger with the Mid-Ulster League in 1990, the League of Women Voters of Dutchess County made a significant impact on the lives of its members and the community.

Early Days of the League in Dutchess County-1920s and 1930s

In 1919, two years after New York State gave women the right to vote, the League of Women Voters of New York State was created to educate women on their new-found rights and to encourage them to get involved in the political process. From its earliest days, the League declared itself a non-partisan organization, not endorsing any political party or candidates, although its members were free to support whoever they chose.

Before the creation of a Dutchess County League of Women Voters, members of The Women's City and County Club of Poughkeepsie participated in the State League convention as delegates in 1921 and as hosts in 1922. Miss Laura Wylie, a Vassar graduate and later head of the English Department, chaired the 1922 convention and led a workshop on "Steps in Civic and Political Education." Miss Marian Dickerman spoke on "Women's Interest in Industrial Affairs," Mrs. Samuel Bens on "Women's Interest in International Affairs" and National League President Mrs. Maud Wood Park on "Recent Achievements in National Legislation for Women."[1] *The Poughkeepsie Eagle News* reported that the convention was "crowded to the doors."[2] Eleanor Roosevelt attended, as did a delegation from Vassar College. Ye Olde Coffee Shoppe at 62 Market Street provided lunch for the participants for 75 cents.

Three years later, in 1925, the Dutchess County League of Women Voters was formed and Mrs. Louise Hill of the Bennett School was elected president. The County League was divided into two districts:

District 1 included Amenia, Pawling, Beacon, Dover, Fishkill, LaGrange, North East, Pine Plains, Pleasant Valley, Red Hook, Wappingers and Washington. Officers were: Anna Vincent Davis of Dover Furnace, Mrs.

YOU ARE INVITED TO THE

DUTCHESS COUNTY CONVENTION

OF THE

LEAGUE OF WOMEN VOTERS

WOMEN'S CITY AND COUNTY CLUB,
62 MARKET ST., POUGHKEEPSIE

Saturday, October 7, 1922

MORNING SESSION

12:00 M.

MRS. GORDON NORRIE, Chairman

Election of County Officers.
Discussion of Congressional District Affairs.

LUNCH

1:00 P. M.

AFTERNOON SESSION

2:00 P. M.

MISS LAURA J. WYLIE, Chairman
Dutchess County Chairman League of Women Voters.

"Steps in Civic and Political Education"
MISS LAURA J. WYLIE

"Women's Interest in International Affairs"
MRS. SAMUEL BENS

"Women's Interest in Industrial Affairs"
MISS MARIAN DICKERMAN

"Recent Achievements in National Legislation for Women"
MRS. MAUD WOOD PARK
President National League of Women Voters

Arrangements have been made with Ye Little Coffee Shoppe at 62
Market St., for the entertainment of members at Luncheon, 75c. Kindly
make reservations with the Club Secretary, by October 5th.

Figure 1. Program from 1922 Convention of the State League of Women Voters held in Poughkeepsie. Adriance Memorial Library Local History Collection, Poughkeepsie, NY.

Joel Spingarn of Amenia, Mrs. Louisa Hill from the Bennett School, Mrs. H. N. Bain of Dover Plains, and Mrs. Henry Morganthau Jr. of Hopewell Junction.

District 2 covered Hyde Park, Staatsburg, and the City and Town of Poughkeepsie. Mary Hinkley of Poughkeepsie was chair; other leaders were Mrs. Fred White, Staatsburg, Marion Whitney of Vassar College, Mrs. M. Burns, Poughkeepsie and Miss Cleona Glass of Poughkeepsie.[3]

On October 3, 1925, Carrie Chapman Catt, a suffragist leader and president of the national League of Women Voters, spoke in Poughkeepsie on "Our International Relations" at a meeting sponsored by the League, the YWCA, AAUW, Federation of Missionary Societies, WCTU, Women' Trade Union League and the Council on Jewish Women. The Honorable Hamilton Fish Jr. presided.[4]

A long-time resident of Dutchess County, Eleanor Roosevelt joined the League of Women Voters in New York City in 1921 and became active on the state level. Throughout the 1920s and 1930s, Mrs. Roosevelt gave frequent speeches, wrote articles, opened her Hyde Park home for fund-raisers and held workshops for the Dutchess County League. She urged women to become active in politics and cited the organization of Dutchess County women as "a model of encouraging women to engage in the political process" in an article written in 1922.[5]

Mrs. Roosevelt was also asked to investigate a charge of fraud at the 1922 state League convention, a charge brought by Staatsburg member Margaret Norrie. The charge was unfounded Mrs. Roosevelt and her team of investigators determined.[6]

In 1930, a Poughkeepsie branch of the League was formed with 50 members. Mrs. Franklin Hemingway was elected chair; Miss Agnes Blair, secretary.[7] Mrs. Roger Elwell chaired a newly formed Beacon branch.

Topics discussed at meetings in the 1930s included a study for a new high school in Poughkeepsie (which would become a reality 25 years later in 1956), the need for a housing authority in Poughkeepsie, world trade and tariffs, and child welfare.[8]

During World War II, the League held meetings to discuss the refugee problem and to examine the Dutchess County Charter.

Sometime in the mid-1940s, the State League withdrew the Poughkeepsie branch's charter because of "strong partisan involvements by members

Figure 2. Miss Cleona Glass, member of City and County Club, elected Secretary of District II of the Dutchess County League of Women Voters in 1925. Photograph. Adriance Memorial Library Local History Collection, Poughkeepsie, NY.

that split the League into Republican and Democratic factions."[9] This author could find no further information on this.

By 1952, the State League gave the Poughkeepsie League provisional status to re-form and reinstated it with full status in 1953. By 1959, membership in the Poughkeepsie League reached a high of 260.

Highlights of League Accomplishments 1952-1990

For the next forty years, the League of Women Voters in Dutchess County persistently pursued its goals of making voting accessible and elections fair, involving citizens in policy making, and improving government. It also served as a training ground for women to enter politics and public service.

Some of the changes the League supported through active lobbying:[10]

- Creation of Dutchess Community College.

- Building a new Poughkeepsie High School.

- Adoption of Permanent Personal Voter Registration in 1964 by the Dutchess County Board of Supervisors after a ten year lobbying effort of League members and several "no" votes by the Board.

- A revised County Charter to create an elected County Executive and County Legislature in place of the Board of Supervisors from the various towns.

- Creation of a Children's Court in Dutchess County in 1961. Judge Joseph Giudice thanked the League for its "interest and foresight" in establishing the court and providing the impetus for the County Board of Supervisors to create legislation.[11] (In 1965, the Children's Court was renamed the Family Court and now has four judges.)

- Creation of the Dutchess County Child Development Commission in 1970 to ensure quality day care services. It is now called the Child Development Council and serves parents, children and day care providers in Dutchess and Putnam Counties.

- Increased access to Adriance Memorial Library in the City of Poughkeepsie for residents of LaGrange and the Town of Poughkeepsie.

- Fair apportionment of county legislative districts.

- Increased public input in the county budget process.

- Support for fair property assessment practices.

- Support for an increased county role in land use planning and public transportation.

A 1963 editorial in the *Poughkeepsie Journal* praised the League for providing

> ...dependable and shrewd leadership in the fight to obtain progressive governmental programs in Dutchess County.... Astute in the conduct of politics, the Women Voters have shown a concern for good government at least equal to that of men and they are moving toward leadership in providing programs for continuing development of our democratic freedoms."[12]

When lobbying proved ineffective in the reapportionment of the county legislature after the 1970 and 1980 census, the League went to court and sued the legislature.

In1970, the League claimed that the multi-district reapportionment plan proposed by the county legislature was unconstitutional. The League gave as an illustration the Town of Poughkeepsie with seven legislators elected at-large had seven voices on the county board, while the City of Poughkeepsie with five districts of one member each would have only one. The League advocated for single-member districts, which were adopted by the County as a result of the lawsuit. Attorneys for the League were Russell Aldrich andWoody Klose; the County was represented by Anthony Quartararo.The League plaintiffs were Jane Gould, Marilyn Schwarz, Elizabeth Schneider, Allyne Rogers, Elayne Weinstein and Joan Jacobs. The court decided in the League's favor by saying the county reapportionment plan was unconstitutional and should be redrawn into single member districts. Walter Jablonski, a political science professor and consultant to the League, said the League showed "great courage in going ahead with a lawsuit" against the prevailing political power.[13]

The 1981 lawsuit filed by the League against the County legislature claimed that the 1980 reapportionment plan approved by the legislature discriminated against minorities and was based on voter registration figures instead of population figures. The League was joined in the lawsuit by the NAACP Legal Defense Fund and eighteen individuals.The New York City law firm Teitellbaum & Hiller handled the case in Federal district court. The case was dismissed until a public referendum was held on the plan. In November 1981, thanks to intensive lobbying by the League and other groups, voters defeated the plan and the legislature had to come up with a new plan of reapportionment before the 1983 elections.

In support of voter information, the League moderated candidates' nights for school boards, town and village boards, county legislative seats and state and national offices. The League worked with the *Poughkeepsie Journal* to publish an election supplement with information on candidates each November. And through public speaking and written materials the League encouraged people of all ages to exercise their civic responsibility to vote.

Leadership Training

An often overlooked contribution of the League of Women Voters was the training of its members to take leadership positions in the community. Many members, this writer included, had joined the League as young mothers with children at home. The League was one of the few organizations that offered baby-sitting at meetings.

Members learned how to carefully study an issue, whether on the local, state or national level, how to come to consensus on action goals, how to plan a strategy for achieving these goals and then advocate for them. This might take the form of testifying at legislative meetings, speaking on the

Esther Schwartz	Peggy Ross	Eleanor Charwat
Margaret Myers	Gail Kressman	Peg Fargo
Alice Howson	Ann Blake	Barbara Heising
Freda Casner	Elayne Weinstein	Elayne Weinstein
Joan Sherman	Jane Gould	Rachel Page
Phyllis Wagner	Allyne Rogers	Peggy Kelland
Anna Buchholz	Eileen Hickey	Brianne Seipp
Lynne Davis	Sandra Zeleznik	Rosealice D'Avanzo

Figure 3. League of Women Voter Presidents 1952-1990.

radio or television, writing editorials or letters to the editor of the newspaper or making phone calls to elected officials.

Although the League has always been non-partisan in not supporting a political party, many members did get involved in political campaigns. As many women reentered the work force in large numbers in the 1970s and 1980s, some women (working or not) decided to run for office. Local League members were successful and were elected on the town, county and state levels, often the first women to hold these positions.

Examples include:

- Anna Buchholz served as Dutchess County legislator (1971-73) and then Poughkeepsie Town Supervisor (1975-1989)
- Lucille Pattison was Dutchess County Executive (1978-1992), the first female in New York State to hold that position
- Eileen Hickey was a New York State Senator (1993-1994)
- Sandra Goldberg served on the Dutchess County Legislature (1982-93; 2004-2011)
- Eleanor Charwat was elected to two terms on the Town of Poughkeepsie Board (1987-1991)

League member Lou Glasse served as Director of the Dutchess County Office of Aging and then as Director of the NY State Office of the Aging (1976-1983). Jane Gould, a former League president, was Lou's deputy in Albany.

Mary Lou Heisenbuttel was selected as the first Executive Director of the Grace Smith House for victims of domestic violence, thanks to her volunteer work and experience at the League.

The League of Women Voters served an important role in Dutchess County and in the lives of its members. Some examples:

Their work on the League natural resources committee helped Anne Conroy and Margery Groten return to the work force for a consulting group on environmental issues.

"My League experience led directly to a job as a lobbyist for arts organizations" said Dare Thompson, past president of the Mid-Hudson League and the State League.

Marianna Martin said "I learned assertiveness training in the League, especially helping with candidates' forums. No other organizations are like the League which is involved in so many issues."

"The League made me aware of the political process as a I moved into a direction as a citizen activist," said Gina Klein."[14]

As League members returned to graduate study or to the workforce, the organization adapted, by changing meeting times to evenings or lunch hours, focusing on fewer issues to study and advocate, holding fewer meetingsand making shorter terms for officers. But even these changes were not enough to maintain membership and recruit leaders. In 1990, the League of Women Voters of Dutchess County disbanded and invited its members to join the Mid-Ulster League. In 2004, that League was renamed the League of Women Voters of the Mid-Hudson Region. As of 2019, 32 of the 142 League members came from Dutchess County.

---

[1]   Program of Convention, Adriance Memorial Library Local History Collection.

[2]   *Poughkeepsie Eagle News*, October 9, 1922.

[3]   Ibid. October 3, 1925, p. 5.

[4]   Ibid.

[5]   Ibid, August 5, 1922.

[6]   Hilda R. Watrous. *In League with Eleanor*, Foundation for Citizen Education, 1984, p.4.

[7]   *Poughkeepsie Eagle News*, June 20, 1930.

[8]   Various issues of *Poughkeepsie Eagle News*.

[9]   *Poughkeepsie Journal*, October 28, 1970.

[10]   *Ballot Box*, Annual Reports and other original documents from League files belonging to Joan Sherman and Eleanor Charwat. Now in Local History Collection at Adriance Memorial Library, Poughkeepsie, NY.

[11]   Letter published in *Ballot Box* publication of Poughkeepsie League of Women Voters, February 1962.

[12]   *Poughkeepsie Journal*, May 16, 1963, p.6.

[13]   Author interview with Walter Jablonski, September 20, 2019.

[14]   All of the above quotes from interviews with the author in 2017-2018.

The Road from Clinton Hollow: A Grandmother's and Granddaughter's Paths to Equal Rights for Women

by Melodye K. Moore

One of the most fascinating things about the study of local history is the serendipitous way in which stories are often revealed. Such was the case when the Dutchess County Historical Society received a small, undated, handmade photograph album in early 2018. The donor, who had been hired to clean out a residence in New Jersey, decided it was better to send it to the Society than "throw it in the dumpster." Eleven photographs depict buildings, residences and landscapes along the road from Salt Point to Clinton Hollow. The inscription "To My Grandmother," followed by "Nina McCulloch" created a tantalizing mystery. Our research transformed the sweet little memento into this story of two extraordinary Dutchess County women. Both grandmother and granddaughter devoted their lives, one long and the other short, to social and civic causes advancing the rights and protections of women and girls in the late nineteenth and early twentieth centuries.

The Clinton Hollow referred to on the cover page of the album that Nina made for her grandmother Ophelia was a small hamlet in the south center of the Town of Clinton. The few homes that formed the community were sprinkled along what are today Schoolhouse, Browning and Clinton Hollow Roads. The Little Wappinger Creek ran through the center. Not a lot has changed over the past century.

Ophelia's Family and Childhood

The Rikert family was one of the earliest to settle the area. On April 16, 1821, Lydia Hodge became Henry Rikert's second wife. Lydia, born in 1798, was 27 years younger than Henry. Four children, Joel, Mary Jane, Martin, and Phebe, would be born to Lydia and Henry between 1822 and 1828. Tragically both Henry and his firstborn, Joel, would die in 1830, reportedly from typhus, leaving Lydia to care for the three remaining children. Eight years later Lydia married Riley Shadbolt. Riley is likely a relative of Israel Shadbolt of Troy who was living in Clinton in 1816 at the time of the birth of his son James. By 1829, he had built a general store at the head of Browning Road and was prominent in public life.[1] In 1831, he ran on the Republican ticket for the State Assembly.[2]

Figure 1. Captioned "The Old Homestead" in the photograph album, this house may be where Ophelia was born and grew up. If not, it is certainly typical of the homes in Clinton Hollow at the time she lived there. Photograph. Nina McCulloch Mattern Photograph Album, Collection of the Dutchess County Historical Society.

Ophelia Shadbolt was born on July 13, 1839 to Lydia and Riley, joining half-siblings that were ten to sixteen years older. Sister Caroline followed two years later when Lydia was 43. Little is known of the couple and their family life but by the time of the 1850 census, Lydia, now 52 was living alone with her five surviving children, ages 8-24. There is no record of where Riley was at this time. Two years later, Lydia died and the Shadbolt girls, thirteen and eleven were left motherless, likely to be raised by their half-sisters. Riley resurfaced in the 1860 census as living in Clinton with the Kittner family.

The only known facts about Ophelia's childhood in Clinton Hollow come from an article she wrote for the May 25, 1936 *Mitchell County Press and Osage News* when she was 97 years old. Despite the hardships of her youth she speaks fondly of her education.

> I was born and reared in the Town of Clinton, Duchess county, on the eastern Part of the state of New York, less than five miles

from where our president, Franklin D. Roosevelt, lives. I attended school in a little white school house, instead of a red one, and as we were always fortunate in having good, intelligent men for trustees; they saw to it that in our school we always had the best teachers that could be obtained.[3]

She goes on to say that the teachers were procured from the City of Philadelphia and, because of the great number of Quakers in Dutchess County, were locally just called "Friends." Describing the teachers as calm, thorough, and understanding of children, Ophelia felt that she had the best of schools for her time. She later claimed that she became a teacher herself at the age of 14, teaching in the county in the spring and fall and coming into Poughkeepsie in the winter for training in the private school that would later be known as Lyndon Hall.

Figure 2. School house No. 5 in Clinton Hollow was where Ophelia was educated and where she stated she later taught. In her memoirs she noted that it was white rather than the normal little red ones. Photograph. Nina McCulloch Mattern Photograph Album, Collection of the Dutchess County Historical Society.

Ophelia, to Iowa

On March 13, 1858, just shy of her twentieth birthday Ophelia married Oscar Maximilliam Amigh. Born in Hillsdale, near Hudson, New York, Oscar was educated at the Amenia Seminary[4] and his marriage certificate states he was a "professor of elocution."[5] After the marriage, Oscar and Ophelia found a suitable house, furnished it and set up housekeeping.

Shortly thereafter, the uncle, who had reared Oscar, died. In her newspaper memoir, Ophelia recounted:

> Now the son (Oscar's cousin) would take control, and husband would be obliged if he remained to have to work for him for a long time. They had not agreed very well and so Mr. Amigh was easily persuaded to go west, which was accomplished by a cousin of his, who had moved to Iowa three years previous.[6]

With little need for a professor of elocution in Clinton Hollow and no desire to work for his step brother-in-law, Oscar announced to his wife "Well, Ophelia, I have decided to go to Iowa, and I will go ahead of you and see how I like it, and also get a place to live in for us when you come." And so, in November, nine months after the marriage, Oscar departed for Iowa leaving an already pregnant Ophelia to follow when he sent for her. For the second time in her young life the most important male figure to her proved to be undependable and unpredictable.

On February 14, 1859, Ophelia left Clinton Hollow for Floyd Centre, Iowa, a trek of over 1,000 miles, which she claimed to make in just one week. In what would become characteristic of Ophelia, she overcame great difficulties to accomplish her goal. Traveling in mid-winter, Ophelia arrived in Janesville, Wisconsin to discover that the only way to cross the river was with horses and wagon on the ice. She described the eleven male passengers traveling with her to be "very kind and did their best to keep her courage up." Having successfully crossed the river, the group landed at McGregor's landing where they found no inn, tavern or hotel to welcome them. Given shelter in a small building, she woke up the next morning to face the task of securing transportation to take her further west. Facing corduroy roads created by freezing and thawing conditions, they used mud wagons pulled by horses that had to be changed every ten miles. Undaunted she procured passage and started on the last leg of her journey.

> I surely found that the truth had been told me, for it required all the ingenuity that I was then mistress of to keep on the seat of the wagon, but I made the best of it and quite early in the evening we reached West Union, where my husband met me and I had the pleasure of his company for the last miles of the journey.[7]

It's hard to know what Oscar was told he would find in Iowa, but he and Ophelia were moving into territory that had only become a state in 1846. Mitchell County where Floyd Centre was located had only been founded in 1851, and it took another two years for the first settler to arrive. Due to the lack of timber on the prairie land, the first houses were covered with new mown grass, followed when possible by log cabins. In 1803 when the territory was purchased, the Sacs, Foxes and Iowa tribes possessed what would become the state. Later migrations brought the Sioux and the Winnabago. Remnants of these earliest tribes still populated the area when the Amighs arrived. Their home was in the midst of both the Sioux and the Winnabago and one quite old Winnabago chief took a liking to the young couple. Frequently on trips past their place he "would come in, go into the kitchen, roll his warm blanket around him, throw himself on the floor and remain until morning, and at break of day, without a word, he would go out and take up his journey."[8] Ophelia stated she was never afraid of him and grew to see him as a protector. On one occasion he interceded in an altercation at their house between a band of young Indians and a traveler passing through on his way to Pike's Peak.

The conditions that greeted Ophelia were not good. The previous year's crops had failed due to heavy and constant rains and, with a new growing season not yet begun, food was alarmingly scarce. During the first six months after her arrival she describes hunger as a constant condition.

> I would go out and gather greens, that grew wild in the fields, and cook them, and then we were obliged to eat them without either salt or vinegar, since the salt was all used up and no more could be brought in until the roads were better. However, we survived.[9]

On July 31, 1859, six months after arriving in Iowa, Ophelia gave birth to a daughter, Mary Eloise.

The Civil War

Life wasn't easy for the young family. In the fall following the birth of Mary, the family suffered from chills and fever. Doctors advised them to leave the farm and, with the help of neighbors, they moved into the village of Floyd Center. The village had no formal school and following the dismissal of the teacher for immoral conduct Ophelia was asked to start a private school which she did. The family later moved to Mitchell where she became the teacher at the village school.[10]

The 1860 census lists Oscar as a farmer in Mitchell County. Just over a month after the outbreak of the Civil War on April 12, 1861, Oscar enlisted as a private in the Union Army.[11] On June 10, he was mustered into the Iowa 3rd Infantry.[12] No record exists to suggest whether Oscar's choice was born of patriotism or a desire to escape the harsh conditions of their new life. Once again Ophelia was faced with her husband leaving home— once again she chose to go with him and joined the Army as a nurse at the age of 23. And, once again, she embarked pregnant on a new chapter in her life. Mary was sent east to her grandmother.

On June 29, 1861, the 3rd Iowa left the state for Hannibal, Missouri with a unit strength of 1,109.[13] By August, the Amighs were at Benton Barracks outside St. Louis, Missouri. The camp, used primarily as a training facility for Union soldiers was where Ophelia gave birth, on August 31, to her second child, Benton B. Amigh, named for his place of birth. Reportedly she went immediately back to the 3rd as a regimental nurse.[14]

While Ophelia's exact duties aren't known, it can be assumed she was dividing her time between field service and service in the hospital in St. Louis, providing comfort and care to the soldiers and especially to those who were sick and wounded. The work was demanding, exhausting and often horrific. Something during these early days of her war efforts aroused in Ophelia the first outward evidence of her innate reform instincts, and she took action by writing a letter on November 1 to another social reformer, Annie Turner Wittenmyer. Like Ophelia, Wittenmyer was an Iowan. Secretary and later General Agent of the Keokuk Soldiers' Aid Society, she traveled extensively to troop encampments to assess conditions and the need for medical supplies and dietary assistance. As her time gathering information in the field grew, so did her influence. Sensing that in Wittenmyer she had found an ally, Ophelia, writing from a hospital in Quincy, Illinois, complained vigorously about the surgeon-in-charge. "Now, Mrs. W, do what you can for us towards removing said Doctor… and the 3rd will bless you forever."[15] Recently, it has been said of Ophelia: "She was an angelic despot who was maybe right, maybe wrong, but never in doubt."[16]

The Battle of First Lexington resulted in hundreds of wounded arriving in St. Louis and the Post and Convalescent Hospitals were established at Benton Barracks. According to the Western Sanitary Commission, conditions there during the winter of 1861–1862 were difficult.

> The presence of so many troops in one great encampment, the crowded condition of the barracks, the inexperience of the soldiers in their first encounter with exposure and hardship, the inclemency of the winter months, and the inability of the department to do all that was required, occasioned a large amount of sickness among the different regiments. The most prevalent diseases were measles, pneumonia, typhoid fever, and diarrhea.[17]

On March 15, 1862, the 3rd Iowa arrived to join the growing federal forces at the Tennessee River opposite Pittsburgh Landing. Oscar and Ophelia were with them, reportedly with their infant son, encamped at Stacy Field adjacent to Hell's Hollow. The Battle of Shiloh began at sunrise on Sunday, April 6 and Ophelia and Oscar were separated.[18] The battle would prove to be one of the bloodiest battles of the war with 13,000 Union and 11,000 Confederate casualties. After Shiloh it was clear that the war would not be won easily or be over quickly and General Ulysses S. Grant, who had led the Union Army, said "I gave up all idea of saving the Union except by complete conquest."[19]

While it's hard to estimate how many women were at Pittsburgh Landing on the battlefield, records prove that Ophelia was there. So was Belle Reynolds. Reynolds, like Ophelia, had followed her husband to war. Reynolds described what the battlefield nurses saw.

> And that operating table!..one by one, they would take from different parts of the hospital a poor fellow, lay him out on those bloody boards, and administer chloroform, but before insensibility, the operation would begin, and in the midst of shrieks, curses, and wild laughs, the surgeon would wield over his wretched victim the glittering knife and saw; and soon the severed and ghastly limb, white as snow and spattered with blood, would fall upon the floor—one more added to the terrible pile."[21]

For days following the battle, Belle and other women, most likely Ophelia among them, walked the battlefield assisting surgeons and ministering to the wounded.[22]

Oscar was one of those wounded during the battle. He survived a gunshot wound but was later described as "never right in the head."[23] Three months later on July 1, 1862, he received a discharge due to disability.[24] It is not known where Oscar spent the remainder of the war, but it has been presumed that Ophelia continued her nursing. It is known that by June of 1863 she was back in St. Louis and on June 8 baby son Benton, not quite two years old, died of whooping cough. Newspaper accounts reported that "The little one was born in Camp Benton, St. Louis, and has ever been the petted child of the 3rd Ia. Inf. Regt. of which both parents were members at the time of his birth. Many brave soldiers mourn his death, for they had wished to see him, like themselves, a true hearted defender of his country."[25] Ophelia's family was further impacted by the war when her half-brother, Martin Rikert, who had enlisted in the 128th NY in late August 1862, died at Ship Island near Baton Rouge, likely of disease.[26]

Ophelia in Poughkeepsie, New York after the Civil War

The details of the Amigh family for the remainder of the war are unknown but their story resurfaces again on January 19, 1866 when their third child, a son, Harrie, was born in Missouri.[27] Towards the end of that year it appears that the marriage between Ophelia and Oscar had broken apart for the St. Louis City Directory lists Oscar living alone at 690 Morgan Street. He is listed as a bookseller.[28] Records seem to indicate that Ophelia had found her way back to Dutchess County with her two surviving children.[29] In Poughkeepsie she directed her reform energies into the Women's Christian Temperance Association and served as the organization's secretary. She was instrumental in the 1874 creation of the Holly Tree Inn that was established by the WCTA on February 11, 1874. The Inn was located on the corner of Main and Clinton Streets and provided lodging and meals to homeless and needy men and boys. A second Inn was quickly established on Main Street below Clover Street and served as centers for promoting both Christianity and temperance. When the operations of the two Inns were suspended by the WCTA in 1876, the Friendly Inn was established to replace them at 469 Main Street and Ophelia became the matron.[30]

At some point Oscar also made his way back home, but the couple did not reunite and census records for 1875, 1880, 1892 and 1900 find Oscar living alone in the Town of Clinton working variously as a farmer, laborer or a trapper. Ophelia did, however, reunite with her father Riley during this time period. In 1870, Riley was living with his step-son, William Rikert, and his family in the Town of Clinton, but by the 1880 census he had relocated to Bellevue Avenue in Poughkeepsie where he was living with Ophelia, her two children, Mary and Harrie, one servant and nine boarders. In 1881, daughter Mary married Robert McCulloch and presumably left her mother's household. It was also during this time period that Ophelia lost her full sister Caroline in 1879 and half-sister Mary Jane in 1881.

It would appear that Ophelia had found in Poughkeepsie plenty of outlets for her reform energies. But something must have been stirring in her and in 1882, perhaps as impulsively as when she followed Oscar to war, she decided to move to Chicago with Harrie, leaving behind her daughter and newborn granddaughter, her father, and her husband. In her later years she suggested that once her children were grown and married she was able to enter upon her great work. [31]

Figure 3. Ophelia Shadbolt Amigh. One of only a handful of photographs of Ophelia, this one was likely taken during her years as the Superintendent of the Illinois State Training School for Delinquent Girls. Date not known, but probably before 1911. Courtesy of the McCulloch Family.

Ophelia off to Chicago to begin "her great work"

The Chicago she found was in the midst of a period of enormous growth, exploding from an 1870 population of 299,000 to nearly 1.7 million in 1900. It was the second largest city in America as well as the fastest growing one. Many of those drawn to the flourishing economy of the city were new immigrants. Not surprisingly the combination of mass immigration and urbanization resulted in massive social changes that were not always good. Reformers recognized the public welfare challenges in Chicago and began to work to address the problems.

It seems clear that by this time Ophelia was a true reformer, but what actually drew her to Chicago? Perhaps it was her battlefield friend Belle Reynolds. Following the war Belle had entered medical school in Chicago, following in the footsteps of her father and brother who were both physicians. Upon graduation she practiced at the Home for the Friendless which had been founded in 1858 to provide social services to women and children.[32] She later served on the staff of the Clinical Society of Hahneman.[33]

Once she arrived in Chicago, it appears that Ophelia became involved with the Erring Women's Refuge.[34] The refuge had been established in 1863 to challenge the legal and social inequity of the double standard of sexual morality that punished women, but not men, for extramarital sexual activities. At the refuge, prostitutes received the support they needed to change their lives. By 1890, the word "Erring" was dropped and the institution became a home for delinquent girls.

Her work at the Erring Women's Refuge was apparently recognized, for when the Illinois State Training School for Delinquent Girls was established in 1893, she was appointed the first superintendent. In 1894, a campus was established on 51 acres of farmland in Geneva, Illinois. The mission of the school was the confinement, education, and reformation of girls between the ages of 10 and 16 years who had been convicted of offenses punishable by law. Ophelia and eight girls moved into the original farmhouse on the property in May of 1895. The following year the first building was constructed. By 1909, the campus had grown to 241 acres and included other cottages and support buildings.[35] It was a correctional facility and girls were locked in their rooms when they were not involved in approved activities such as school, working, or attending church. The goal was to rehabilitate the girls so that they could return to productive lives in society.

Ophelia became a well known and well respected leader in the field of social reform and justice for delinquent girls. In 1904, the *Historical Encyclopedia of Illinois* included a tribute to Ophelia in its "History of Kane County." "Under Mrs. Amigh's management this school has become one of the noted educational and reformatory institutions of the State." She traveled the country sharing her views on the causes of delinquency. In Woodstock, Illinois in January of 1906, she spoke to an assembly of teachers and gave a "soul stirring address on "Degenerate Girls" tracing the chief causes to the use of alcohol by parents or ancestors."[36] She wrote extensively on the topic and authored a chapter in Ernest Bell's 1910 book, *Fighting The Traffic In Young Girls or War On The White Slave Trade*. Two years later Jane Addams published *New Conscience and an Ancient Evil* that explored the same issues raised by Ophelia—prostitution and the white-slave traffic. Although today's historians believe the extent of the problem was exaggerated, at the time the issue was seen as a huge problem. Ophelia and Addams were both listed as contributors to the *Star* issue of the *The Women's World*, in February 1909—Addams as the author of an article entitled " Wolves That Pray on Women" and Ophelia as the author of "A Word About Wayward Girls."[37]

As the years went on, Ophelia's ferocity in fighting against what she felt were the causes that led young girls to become delinquent became almost evangelical. In her biennial reports to the state, she described the conditions in which the girls had lived before coming to her; she lobbied for equal treatment for girls; and she called out crooked judges.[38] "She might be right, she might be wrong, but she was never in doubt." One can imagine that compromise was not acceptable to her. It was perhaps inevitable that her positions would eventually lead to her dismissal.

Ophelia Amigh Ousted at Training School

On June 30, 1911, the headline in the Chicago Tribune read" Mrs. Amigh Ousted At Training School." The request for her resignation after eighteen years of service was made by the state board of administration upon her return from a vacation in Poughkeepsie. "Mrs. Amigh was greatly surprised yesterday when she received the letter from the board." Ophelia alleged that no reason for the board's actions was stated in the letter and a request for a hearing was denied. The article went on to say "Her administration of affairs is said to have been satisfactory all these years, but recently politics, it is alleged, entered the affairs of the institution in a more rampant manner than formerly and as a result there has been a general shaking up. It is charged that certain politicians are replacing the ousted officials and employees with some of their particular friends."

On July 8, an article in the *Inter Ocean* reported that on July 7 the state board issued a statement explaining that the resignation request had been made for: purchasing furniture without lawful right; awarding contracts without competition; use of the "strong chair" and use of a rawhide in punishing girls. On July 23 in the Sunday edition of the *Inter Ocean*, Ophelia declared all charges to be false and offered explanations for the allegations made against her. She concluded her remarks by saying "I have made no comments in a spirit of criticism. I have given the girls as near as possible a mother's care and guidance, and it remains for those who have done but little or no work of this kind and who never put a foot into this institution to break down its usefulness to a great extent."

Ophelia's Return to Poughkeepsie, 1911, then on to Alabama in 1912

In 1911, Ophelia had been in Chicago for 29 years. A lot had happened to her during that time. On a personal level, Ophelia's father Riley joined her in Chicago sometime prior to 1888 when he appears on the Chicago Voter Registration list. Also in 1888, son Harrie, who had come with her from Poughkeepsie, married and, in 1889, had relocated to Seattle where he became an engineer with a fire company. Tragically Harrie died in 1891 at the age of 25 from an internal hemorrhage.[39] Eight years later in

1898, Riley would also die, leaving Ophelia alone with her work. Now, her life's work had been taken from her and once again she had to find a new beginning.

She returned to Poughkeepsie to find that new beginning and once again threw herself into welfare work. By November, she was President of the Women's Christian Temperance Union and, by February of 1912, she was lobbying for the WCTU to open a detention center for wayward women and young girls in their Cannon Street building.[40] Mayor Sague and other city officials were less than enthusiastic about the plans and some suggested they were not convinced of her management skills.[41] In the end it didn't matter, for on August 31, 1912, it was reported that she had been selected to be the Superintendent of the Alabama State School for Girls, near Eastlake in Birmingham, taking up her duties at the age of 74. She continued in the position for another ten years and upon her retirement she became a parole officer. In 1914, Hastings Hornell Hart, a noted prison authority, children's advocate and one time superintendent of the Illinois Children's Home and Aid Society declared Mrs. Amigh to be "the first great pioneer leader in the United States in the work of reclaiming girls."[42] In 1927, at age 88 she was a delegate to the National Conference of Social Work in Des Moines, Iowa. It was the fiftieth annual conference that she had attended and she was the oldest delegate.[43] A year later she gave up active work.

Figure 4. Portrait image of Ophelia, age, 76, when she was the Superintendent of the Alabama Home of Refuge. The image was included in the 1915 Report of the Board of Managers. Photo courtesy of the Alabama Department of Archives and History. Donated by Alabama Media Group.

The Birmingham News of Wednesday, July 13, 1938 included a feature story about Ophelia describing her as "Active and Alert As She Nears 100 Mark." The reporter who interviewed her for the story remarked on the many birthday greetings which came from "her girls," and commented that during her time as superintendents in both Illinois and Alabama 15,000 young women had passed under her care and guidance. During the interview, Ophelia spoke of Mary, her only child, now a white-haired woman of 79 who had been blind for many years and noted it was enough for her granddaughter and great-grandchildren in New York to look after "one old lady" so she remained in Birmingham to be administered to by beloved strangers.

On January 31, 1939, five months shy of her 100th birthday, Ophelia Shadbolt Amigh died. The February 3rd edition of the *Birmingham Press* said of her funeral, "Mother Amigh, As True Soldier, Is Buried With Military Honors." Described as Birmingham's oldest social worker, she was laid to rest in Forest Hill Cemetery and Alabama had its first military funeral for a Civil War nurse. Hundreds of "daughters" were said to have come to weep at her bier. The flag waved at half staff, members of the Gorgas Number 1 Post of the American Legion paid tribute, and volleys were sounded. "Farewell my comrade, a legionnaire said. A red rose was laid tenderly upon the bier. Taps sounded. And Mrs. Amigh had gone to join her husband in the Great Beyond."

Nina Mattern, Granddaughter of Ophelia Amigh

Ophelia lived to be nearly 100 years old. Her granddaughter, creator of the album would die prematurely in 1918, twenty-one years before the death of her grandmother. The album itself indicates a fondness between the two women and Nina's blossoming commitment to women's issues and concerns speaks to the influence that Ophelia must have had on her granddaughter.

Nina McCulloch was the first born child of Ophelia's daughter Mary Eloise and her husband Robert. Nina was born on October 17, 1882, the year Ophelia left for Chicago. The photograph album says Nina was born in Clinton Hollow but the family later moved to Poughkeepsie. Brother Fred was born in 1885 and sister Ruth in 1892. Little is known about her childhood. On June 22, 1900 at the Collingwood Opera House she was one of 28 graduates of Poughkeepsie High School. Her senior essay was entitled "The Pessimist."[44] Sometime before 1910, she married William C. Mattern and they were living on Hammersley Avenue. Nina and William

Figure 5. Nina McCulloch Mattern. This photograph graces the cover of the photograph album given to Ophelia by her granddaughter Nina. Date: before 1918. Although the woman in the carriage is not identified, it is highly likely that the subject is Nina McCulloch Mattern. Nina McCulloch Mattern Photograph Album, Collection of the Dutchess County Historical Society.

were both members of the Poughkeepsie Club, a musical group that presented operas.

Within a few years the *Poughkeepsie Eagle* newspaper started reporting on her suffrage activities. The March 20, 1914 *Poughkeepsie Eagle* noted that she was a featured speaker at a suffrage tea and spoke on current events in the movement. In part, she spoke of a large suffrage meeting in Birmingham convened to organize suffrage workers in the south. Likely the information came from her grandmother. At the Women's Independence Day Celebration in Eastman Park in May of the same year she read the Suffrage Resolutions.[45] On June 25, under Rhinebeck news, it was reported that a woman suffrage meeting would be held on the high school grounds and that Nina Mattern would be one of the speakers. On October 26, 1915, it was reported that she, along with Edward S. Van Zile of New York

City, were speakers at a suffrage meeting in Memorial Hall in Pine Plains. Talks like these were undoubtedly part of the lead up to the upcoming November 2 New York State election that included a referendum on the suffrage issue. Despite widespread lobbying, the referendum failed with 57 % of the voters saying no.

Nina, along with other suffragists, wasted no time in getting the fight moving again and on February 4, 1916, she was present at an all day conference on suffrage at the Poughkeepsie Court House with other prominent local leaders such as Margaret Lewis Gordon Norrie of Staatsburg and Amy Spingarn of Amenia.

The Poughkeepsie Suffrage Party kicked off 1917 with a Suffrage Tea on February 21. Nina was among the featured speakers and delivered an eloquent explanation of what getting the vote meant to her. "She spoke of the tendency to lay too much stress upon the vote itself and not enough on the struggle for women to set the standards for women, the standards which heretofore have been set by men."[46] She didn't just want the right to vote, she wanted women to be treated equally and have control over their own destiny. Her grandmother Ophelia, whom she probably got to know when she returned to Poughkeepsie from Chicago in 1911, certainly was an example of a woman who chose to take her life in her own hands. It's likely she inspired Nina to see that women could be masters of their own fate.

World War I and the Canning Club

1917 proved to be a watershed year for the country and for women in New York State. On April 6, Congress declared war on Germany. Many suffragists like Nina felt compelled to support the war effort while not losing sight of their goal to see voting rights for women passed in the fall election. The April 9 edition of the *Poughkeepsie Eagle* reported on the "Campaign To Produce Larger Crops in Dutchess." At a conference held in Poughkeepsie that included members of the Farm Bureau, the Chamber of Commerce, and the Agricultural Society, Nina, who was by now the secretary of the Suffrage Party, announced that a "plan had been set afoot for enlisting the aid of the housewives of the county in a canning club." Proof that the canning club was up and running was documented in a four minute film showing Nina and her sister teaching women to can.[47] After local showings, the film played nationally. The *Evening Enterprise* reported that Dutchess County was the first county in the state to organize its women for food production. Further evidence of the need for women to balance their support of the war with their unflinching drive for the vote is seen on the sign attached to the back of the car seen driving away at the end of the film —"Suffrage War Service."

On November 6, 1917, women won the right to vote in New York State. The Poughkeepsie Suffrage Party was successful in carrying the vote whereas elsewhere in Dutchess those against the referendum were in the majority. Statewide however, women had finally reached their goal. With the vote won, local women who had been engaged in the suffrage movement moved on to educating women about contemporary political affairs and how they could engage. In January of 1918, Nina went to New York City where she attended a Normal Class for teachers on citizenship sponsored by the Suffrage Party.[48] On her return, it was reported she would take an active role in educating women voters. In September, she took what she had learned and presented at the Conference of Women Voters, speaking in Poughkeepsie on election problems related to the methods of registration for cities and rural districts.[49]

1918 would also be a year where Americans experienced great joy and great sorrow. The gradual return of the American soldiers from the trenches of France following the November 11 armistice would reunite many families and put an end to the war to end all wars. The joy was overshadowed however by the fact that world was in the midst of a global flu pandemic commonly called the Spanish Flu. First observed in Kansas in January of 1918, by March it had reached Queens and by October the *Poughkeepsie Eagle* reported the "Flu Still Holds City In Its Grip." Health officials were already overseeing two emergency hospitals and looking to open a third at the Masonic Temple on Cannon Street.

There was a dire need for nurses and, following in the footsteps of her grandmother, Nina volunteered and was put in charge of the Masonic Temple Hospital.[50] Sadly, unlike her grandmother, Nina did not survive her volunteer service, dying on October 31, 1918, twenty five days after her brother Fred's death from the same virus. The newspapers reported that she had labored night and day until she became so tired she was ordered to take a complete rest by her physician, Dr. J. Wilson Poucher.[51] Her many accomplishments were cited in the newspaper—one of the first and most prominent workers for suffrage in Poughkeepsie, a founder of the Women's City Club, Executive Director of the Women's Branch of the Home Defense League, and fundraiser for the Women's Land Army. On Monday, November 18, the Women's City Club met and the first part of the meeting was turned over to tributes in her honor. Miss Laura Wylie, chairman of the club said of her:

She saw life so humanly and she was one of the best of demo-
crats, for she really lived democracy. Mrs. Mattern observed no
distinctions except those of personality and character. She was
full of information and real philosophy and, with her vigor and
directness of mind, had a better understanding of current events
than most of us.[52]

Mrs. Gordon Norrie also paid a tribute saying "There was no person in this
county who did more to bring suffrage to the women than Mrs. Mattern."
The City Club passed a resolution saying

Her vision of the larger fields of usefulness which women were
to enter when the franchise had been extended to them—a vision
inherited in part from her grandmother, Mrs. Amigh—made her
eager to place herself on record as a firm believer in the cause
when the suffrage movement received its first impetus in Poughkeepsie in the spring of 1909.The fact that there were years
ahead before the vote could be won did not for a moment turn
her aside from the goal in view.

Conclusion

For now, it's not known how much time Ophelia and Nina spent together as grandmother and granddaughter. Ophelia regularly visited Poughkeepsie after leaving in 1882, the year of Nina's birth, and she returned
briefly to Poughkeepsie when she left Chicago. During these visits, did
they take the drive from Poughkeepsie, where they both lived, to Clinton
Hollow, where they were both born? Did they talk about overcoming life's
difficulties, about standing up for what one believes in no matter the con-
sequences, and about making sacrifices in the service of others? Did they
recognize that they shared a relentless will to overcome life's obstacles and
keep moving forward? Ophelia lived a remarkable 99 years and got up and
persevered whenever she encountered adversity. Nina died shortly after
her 36th birthday. What might she have achieved had she been granted
the longevity of her grandmother? Each woman, by any standard, was
remarkable in her own right. But, as grandmother and granddaughter,
each woman lived through periods of seismic changes in American life—
westward expansion, the Civil War, the Progressive Movement, the fight
for National Suffrage for Women, World War I and the Spanish Flu—and
they made the conscious choice to be participants and agents of change
rather than bystanders.

Postscript: As this article is being published Ophelia's great-great-grand-
son, Darcy McCulloch, is completing a rough draft of a book about her.

His in depth and ongoing research has revealed much more information about her life, her character and her lifelong devotion to social justice. DCHS will notify its members when the book has been printed and is available for purchase.

---

1   William P. McDermott, "Clinton, Dutchess County, New York, A History of A Town," (Clinton Corners: Town of Clinton Historical Society, 1987), p. 164.

2   *Poughkeepsie Journal* (November 9, 1831), p. 3.

3   "War Nurse, 97, Tells of Early History—Civil War Service," Ophelia Amigh," *Mitchell County Press and OsageNews* (May 25, 1936). See also *Birmingham News* (February, 1, 1939), p. 18.

4   19th Annual Catalogue of The Officers and Students of Amenia Seminary for 1854," (Amenia: 1855), not paginated.

5   "Rikert, Rykert, Riker: A Record of the Descendants of Joseph Rikert,: Ancestry.com.

6   "War Nurse, 97, Tells of Early History—Civil War Service," Ophelia Amigh," *Mitchell County Press and OsageNews* (May 25, 1936).

7   Ibid.

8   Ibid.

9   Ibid.

10   Ibid.

11   "Roster and Records of Iowa Soldiers In The War of Rebellion, National Archives: Index To Federal Pension Records," Ancestry.com.

12   "Third Iowa Volunteer Infantry Regiment," Wikipedia, last edited February 11, 2020.

13   Shilohdiscussiongroup, posted Dec. 31, 2016 by Rbn3.

14   Elizabeth D. Leonard, *Yankee Women: Gender Battles In The Civil War* (New York: W.W. Norton and Co.; 1994), p. 59.

15   Shilohdiscussiongroup, posted Jan. 6, 2017 by Rbn3.

16   www.thecivilwarmuse.com/index.php?page=benton-barrack, retrieved Feb. 16, 2020.

17   Shilohdiscussiongroup.

18   www.thecivilwarmuse.com/index.php?page=benton-barrack, retrieved Feb. 16, 2020.

[19] Civil War Book of Days Archive, constantcontact.com/fs013/1102264498897/archive/1109706655158.html.

[20] Shiloh discussion group, posted Jan. 6, 2017 by Rbn3.

[21] Ibid.

[22] Cliff McCarthy, "Women In The Valley, Belle Loomis (Macomber) Reynolds," https://pvhn2.word press.com/1800-2belle-loomis-macomber-reynolds.

[23] Shiloh discussion group, posted Jan. 6, 2017 by Rbn3.

[24] U.S. Civil War Records and Profiles, 1861–1865, Ancestry.com. U.S. Civil War Records and Profiles, 1861–1865, Ancestry.com.

[25] Charles City Intelligencer (July 2, 1863), cited in Shilohdiscussiongroup.

[26] "Rikert, Rykert, Riker: A Record of the Descendants of Joseph Rikert, Ancestry.com.

[27] Ibid.

[28] *St. Louis City Directory* (1866), p. 195.

[29] *Poughkeepsie Eagle-News* (March 13, 1933), p.2.
Ibid.

[30] *Birmingham News* (May 3, 1914), p. 10.

[31] Michael Redmon, "Question: Belle Reynolds (Santa Barbara Independent, June 5, 2008).

[32] Belle Reynolds, Wikipedia, last edited March 8, 2020, retrieved Feb. 22, 2020.

[33] Ophelia L. (Shadbolt) Amigh Message Board, Biographies, Ancestry.com, June 9, 1999, retrieved April 12, 2018.

[34] Susan Cherney, " Illinois State Training School For Delinquent Girls – A Short History" (Neighbors of Geneva Magazine, 2011),, p.38.

[35] *Woodstock Sentinel*, (January, 18, 1906), p. 2.

[36] The "Woman's World," may have been a magazine insert. It appeared in the Saturday Evening Post, Vol. 181, Issue 2, 1909; and *Lippincott's Monthly Magazine*, Vol. 83, 1909.

[37] Related to the author by the great-nephew of Ophelia who had researched her original biennial reports. The comments reflect his interpretation of why she was dismissed.

[38] *Seattle Post-Intelligencer* (November 22, 1891), p. 8.

[39] *Poughkeepsie Daily-Eagle* (February 14, 1912), p. 6.

[40] *Poughkeepsie Daily-Eagle* (March 6, 1912), p. 5.

[41] *Birmingham News* (May 3, 1914), p.10.

[42] *Des Moines Tribune* (May 14, 1927), p. 11.

[43] *Poughkeepsie Eagle-News* (June 22, 1900), p. 6.

[44] *Poughkeepsie Eagle-News* (May 5, 1914), p. 6.

[45] *Poughkeepsie Eagle-News* (February 21, 1917), p. 5.

[46] "The Latest Kinks In Canning," Bray Studios, 1917, Courtesy of the George Eastman Museum.

[47] *Poughkeepsie Eagle-News* (January 28 1918), p. 6.

[48] *Poughkeepsie Eagle-News* (September 20, 1918), p. 2.

[49] *Poughkeepsie Eagle-News* (November 1, 1918), p. 3.

[50] Ibid.

[51] *Poughkeepsie Eagle-News* (November 19, 1918), p. 2.

[52] Ibid.

Amy Spingarn: Humility and Pride

by Camille Roccanova

It is mid-August, 1914, in Amenia, New York. Women in headbands and long, white Grecian dresses parade across the lawn of Troutbeck, the Spingarns' country estate.

The line of women—members of the Dutchess County Woman Suffrage Association—squint in the sun, smile, and talk amongst themselves. A crowd looks on, the men in boater hats and starched white shirts, the women with parasols and crisp summer dresses.

Figure 1. Woman Suffrage pageant during the Amenia Field Day at Troutbeck, 1914. Amy Spingarn collection, Amenia Historical Society.

The crowd watches as a pageant unfolds: A young girl kneels, hands bound, at the feet of a woman wearing a crown and a dress covered in stars (Figure 1). The crowned woman holds a shield that bears the name "New York" along with an oversized question mark, effectively demanding to know when the state will honor women's right to vote. Somewhere in the watching crowd is Amy Spingarn, mistress of Troutbeck and one of the many women that those who create history often choose to overlook—the ones that made history but did so behind the scenes.

"...And then I found I too had flames"[1]

Born Amy Einstein on January 29, 1883, she was a painter, poet, patron of the arts and a leader in the women's suffrage movement. She died at the age of ninety-seven on June 25, 1980, having lived through more history than most, from the advent of the automobile to the enfranchisement of women, from the dawning of the twentieth century to the waging of both World Wars and the war in Vietnam.

The daughter of a wealthy businessman, Amy grew up in a world of ease, comfort, and restriction that she was eager to—and eventually did—escape from. "All thru [sic] my childhood I seethed with inner rebellion," she wrote in an unusually personal paper that she presented to the Analytical Psychology Club of New York, "I hated my imprisoned life, and my greatest wish was to be free of my family and free to discover what life was really like for myself; in my own terms and not my mother's. It might be hard but it would be interesting and challenging and anything would be better than my lifeless stagnation..."[2]

In early twentieth-century New York, even her privilege did not give her the social currency she needed to realize this wish. After studying in Europe and at Barnard College, she met and later proposed to Columbia University literature professor, Joel Spingarn (1875–1939), and they married on December 21, 1905. After he was dismissed from Columbia in 1911, Joel went on to cofound Harcourt, Brace and Company, and became a literary critic, horticulturalist (he had the world's largest collection of clematis), and president of the NAACP board. A passionate advocate of social justice, he introduced her to—or gave her the means to become involved with—women's suffrage, the civil rights movement and the NAACP, and the New York art world, from the Harlem Renaissance to the galleries of Manhattan.

In 1907, the Spingarns purchased Troutbeck; it came with its own pedigree. Originally the home of the Benton family, it was where poet John Burroughs is said to have first read *Leaves of Grass*. And it was here that they hosted the Amenia Field Day every August from 1910 to 1914, a "rural experiment in 'co-operative recreation,'"[3] of which the suffrage parade and pageant were a part. Amy had spent several years as an active member of the suffrage movement, particularly in Dutchess County, giving speeches, attending meetings in Poughkeepsie, selling flowers in New York City to raise money, and convincing the influential men she knew to support women's right to vote—a task she hated. "How I loathed asking some of the men I have spoken to this last week to 'vote for the ladies.' It soiled me...," she wrote to Joel. It was ultimately worth doing, however: "[N]ow I'll never have to do it again...I really feel a new self respect. I didn't think I would feel that way about it—." She signed the letter, "with love from your enfranchised Amy."[4]

Amy kept a journal detailing her work in the suffrage movement, writing responses to common arguments about why women shouldn't be able to vote ("Neglect of Home" and "Duplication of Vote") and listing what good they would do with the vote ("better salaries," "better laws," and "street cleaning (dead horse story)." "We make no promises but why should we?" she wrote. "No one asks the boy of 21 what he will do with the ballot."[5]

She was at her most powerful and persuasive in a 1915 speech, when she responded to the common refrain that women are too emotional to be given equal rights or political power—one that is still, unfortunately, familiar today:

> [E]motion is not the attribute of one sex alone, men and women alike possess it, and its absence cannot be made a requirement for voting...well-directed indignation is a mighty lever for good. The lives of women are so shaped that they, even more than men, possess it in a form most useful for the public good."[6]

Before the 19th Amendment was passed in 1920, women's right to vote was ratified by New York State in 1917. The New York Right to Vote law was accomplished after years of hard, unpaid work, and after it failed to pass in the two previous years. Amenia's neighbors, Northeast, Dover, and Pawling, did vote to in favor of women's voting rights in 1916, but Amenia itself—Amy's district—resoundingly did not. (They did, however, vote "wet" in greater numbers than ever before, making their priorities very clear.)

"...these beautiful days of understanding"

Almost exactly two years after the 1914 Field Day, and on the very same Troutbeck lawn, another group gathered from August 24 to 26, 1916: a contingent of prominent civil rights leaders, meeting for the first of two historic Amenia Conferences (Figure 3). At the completion of this 1916 meeting, the plan was to have a meeting every year thereafter. However, World War I crushed this idea and the next historic meeting was not held until 1933, again at Troutbeck. "[T]hese beautiful days of understanding," one of its most well known attendees, W.E.B. Du Bois, called it.[7] Other attendees included Mary B. Talbert, a suffragist and one of the founders of the Niagara movement, and Inez Milholland, lawyer and suffragist (only months before her death at the age of 30). The NAACP had been formed only seven years earlier, in 1909, and was often criticized for being run by

Figure 2. Members of the NAACP at the 1916 Conference held at Troutbeck in Amenia, New York, the country home of Joel and Amy Spingarn. W.E.B. Du Bois was present as was John Milholland, then treasurer of the organization. Inez Milholland, his daughter and renowned suffragist was also present. 1916. Photograph. Library of Congress, Prints & Photographs Division, Visual Materials from the NAACP Records.

outsiders with their own interests at heart, not those of the black community. However, this first conference was successful, dismantling old rivalries, uniting NAACP members and others to a common purpose, and ultimately helping the NAACP become a powerful national organization.

Both Joel and his brother, Arthur B. Spingarn, had been involved with the NAACP from its early days. Joel was elected board chairman in 1915, and served as president from 1929 until his death in 1939. However, Amy rarely appears in histories of the NAACP, despite her decades-long support. And although she took over her husband's place on the board of directors after his death, her husband's name remains synonymous with the organization, while hers does not. The *Troutbeck Press*, started and run by Amy, printed a pamphlet on the Amenia Conference, written by W.E.B. Du Bois. In it, the only mention of Amy perfectly expresses both her commitment to social causes and her presence in the historical record—quietly helping, not getting credit, always observing: "Mrs. Spingarn strolled over now and then and looked at us quietly and thoughtfully."[8]

"What else does life impose on wives and mothers?"[9]

Amy gave birth to and began raising four children within the first five years of her marriage, a physically and emotionally taxing job (Figure 3). Having left behind her isolated, restricted upbringing, she now turned to art—painting, printmaking, and poetry—to express new feelings of confinement. Being a wife was like being in "a garden / with walls around it; No woods or fields / To wander or stray in."[10] And raising children did not come naturally to her: "Some gardeners / Nurse their plants / With loving care, / But I am an impatient gardener / Who takes little joy / In tending hers."[11] (That Joel was an avid horticulturalist gives an added layer of depth to these analogies.)

Figure 3. Amy Spingarn and her children, n.d. Photograph. Amy Spingarn Collection, Amenia Historical Society.

It is no surprise then that she later developed an interest in the birth control movement. Very little record remains of her efforts, though it is likely she became involved through her friendship with Beatrice Hinkle, a psychoanalyst and member of the Heterodoxy Club, with which Margaret Sanger was also involved.[12] Regardless, it was something she was passionate about; Amy's daughter, Hope, recalls her bringing back "exotic contraceptives" from a trip to Europe and giving them to her and her friend.[13]

In 1932, Spingarn studied with one of the most influential artists and teachers of the twentieth century, Hans Hofmann, whom she and Joel helped leave Germany in 1930. She also learned how to set type and carve woodblocks, skills which she used to create the Troutbeck Press. The magazine later published poet Langston Hughes's Dear Lovely Death with a frontispiece by Spingarn. The title poem was read at both hers and Joel's funerals; at hers it was read out as her ashes were sprinkled into the stream at Troutbeck.[14]

Amy Spingarn is credited by historians Carla Kaplan and Barbara Joyce Rossas spearheading the 1935 exhibition "An Art Commentary on Lynching."[15] She also provided financial support and the prize money. Though it failed to generate support for anti-lynching legislation, it was a shocking and thought-provoking show.

Unlike many women connected to the Harlem Renaissance, Spingarn spent little time in uptown Manhattan. Her relationships with the black artists of the day were more professional than personal, largely consisting of artistic patronage. However, like Nancy Cunard and Charlotte Osgood Mason—some of the white women of the Harlem Renaissance collectively called "Miss Anne"—Amy found escape and expression in the lives and work of black artists of the day, forming relationships complicated by race, class, and privilege. She is best known for her support of the poet Langston Hughes, with whom she corresponded for more than forty years, from 1925 to 1967. He was one of the many influential "poets, artists, intellectuals, and activists of the day—including George Washington Carver, James Weldon Johnson, Zora Neale Hurston, and Carl Jung—whose portrait she drew.

"Some weeks ago I had a very interesting dream..."[16]

The foundation of her portraits and poetry was her interest in psychology, particularly the teachings of Jung. She was an active member of the Analytical Psychology Club of New York, and a patient and correspondent of Carl Jung. She attended two of his seminars (Swanage, England, 1925;

Figure 4. Amy Spingarn and Carl Jung, Bailey Island, Maine, 1936. Photograph. Box 15, Folder 1, Joel E. Spingarn papers, Manuscripts and Archives Division, The New York Public Library.

Bailey Island, Maine, 1936) and traveled to Zurich in 1928 to undergo analysis with him. And while she corresponded periodically with him from 1925 to 1959, there are few extant letters (See her in the photograph, Figure 4. She and Carl Jung are on a porch in Maine. Yet Amy hovers at the edge, almost completely out of view. She is holding a camera, apparently preferring to see, rather than be seen.)

Fellow Analytical Psychology Club member Dorsha Hayes said in her memorial speech: "Amy was one of the few persons on this continent to know the work of Jung in the early days of this century; she was a Jungian before any Jungian societies had been formed."[17]

"Dear lovely death, change is thy other name." [18]

After Joel's death in 1939, Amy split her time between her apartment in New York City and her home at Troutbeck, and also traveled to Haiti, Iceland, Ecuador, and throughout Europe. While she outlived her husband by thirty-three years, his papers in archival collections, such as the New York Public Library, far outnumber hers. Those that do exist—letters, drawings, translations, photographs, and ephemera—are found mostly within the collections of other people. Most of her letters at the New York Public Library date from 1916 to 1919, when Joel was serving in the military. A small number are from after his death, and most relate to a biography that Ph.D. student Martin Van Deusen was writing on Joel. Her many travels remain largely undocumented. The hundreds of letters she must have written after Joel's death are, almost entirely, a mystery.

Amy's letters were catalogued as part the Joel E. Spingarn papers at the New York Public Library in 1976, not long after the emergence of women's history as an academic field (thanks to the likes of feminist author and historian Gerda Lerner). It was a time when women's lives and stories were usually consigned to a lesser space within their husband's papers. Perhaps the clearest lack of her presence in history is that even Wikipedia still doesn't have a page for her.

Did she purposefully stay out of the spotlight, as historian Carla Kaplan suggests?[19] Were her relative silence and invisibility intentional acts, meant to distance herself from being categorized simply as a wealthy white woman who enjoyed financing the work of black artists? Certainly, she felt conflicted, pulled between her ambitions and what people expected of her as a married woman with children. Whatever her intentions, the lack of respect and attention paid to her—both during her lifetime and after—have erased her name from much of history.

In an article about proper, well-behaved women, historian Laurel Thatcher Ulrich wrote the immortal sentence: "Well-behaved women seldom make history."[20] The Amy who exists in archives lacks the attributes often associated with compelling historical characters. Polite, measured, she was not overly rebellious or rude or eccentric. She did not put her desires above those of others, nor forsake her family for an art career. And yet, she persists—in the archives of other people's lives, in the footnotes of books—waiting, patiently, to have her say.

---

[1] I would like to thank the New York Public Library, from whom I received a fellowship in 2019 that helped me pursue my research on Amy Spingarn. Amy Spingarn, "The Parlor Car, II" in *Humility and Pride* (New York, NY: Harcourt Brace, 1926), p. 20.

[2] Amy Spingarn, "Mermaids" (Unpublished typescript of paper given to the Religion and Philosophy Group of the Analytical Psychology Club of NY, April 24, 1951, collection of the Kristine Mann Library), p. 2.

[3] Pamphlet for the Amenia Field Day, 1913, MssCol 2846, Box 17, Folder 1, Joel E. Spingarn papers, Manuscripts and Archives Division, The New York Public Library, New York, NY.

[4] Correspondence from Amy Spingarn to Joel Spingarn, undated, MssCol 2846, Box 13, Folder 4, Joel E. Spingarn papers, Manuscripts and Archives Division, The New York Public Library, New York, NY.

[5] Journal entries, Amy Spingarn collection, undated, Amenia Historical Society, Amenia, NY.

[6] Ibid.

[7] W.E. Burghardt DuBois, "The Amenia Conference: An Historic Negro Gathering," 1916, pp. 17–18, Ms 1824, Box 4, Folder 4, Donald C. Brace papers, Rare Book and Manuscript Library, Columbia University Library, New York, NY. See also Julia Hotton, "The Second Annual N.A.A.C.P. Meeting, Amenia, N.Y., *Dutchess County Historical Society 2017 Yearbook* 96 (Poughkeepsie, NY: Dutchess County Historical Society, 2017) pp. 73-78; and Candace J. Lewis, "Inez: Icon of a Movement," *Dutchess County Historical Society 2017 Yearbook* 96 (Poughkeepsie NY: Dutchess County Historical Society, 2017), pp. 79-96.

[8] W.E. Burghardt DuBois, pp. 13–14.

[9] Amy Spingarn, "Wives and Mothers" in *Humility and Pride* (New York, NY: Harcourt Brace, 1926), p. 64.

[10] Ibid., p. 64.

[11] Ibid., p.63.

[12] Jay Sherry, "Beatrice Hinkle and the Early History of Jungian Psychology in New York," *Behav Sci (Basel)* 3, no. 3 (2013): 492–500, doi:10.3390/bs3030492.

[13] Michele Birnbaum, *Race, Work, and Desire in American Literature, 1860–1930*, (New York, NY: Cambridge University Press, 2003), p. 183n59.

[14] Ibid., p. 107

[15] Carla Kaplan, *Miss Anne in Harlem* (New York, NY: HarperCollins, 2013), p.377–78n80.

[16] Correspondence from Amy Spingarn to Carl Jung, undated, Hs 1056:27213, Jung, Carl Gustav (1875-1961), Psychiater Und Psychologe; Privatdozent Der Universität Zürich, Titularprofessor Der ETH, Professor Der Universität Basel: Wissenschaftlicher Nachlass.

[17] Dorsha Hayes, "In Memoriam," *Bulletin of the Analytical Psychology Club of New York* 42, no. 6:5.

[18] Langston Hughes, "Dear Lovely Death" in Dear Lovely Death (New York, NY: Troutbeck Press), 1931.

[19] Carla Kaplan, *Miss Anne in Harlem* (New York, NY: HarperCollins, 2013), p. xxii.

[20] Laurel Thatcher Ulrich, *Well-Behaved Women Seldom Make History* (New York, NY: Vintage Books, 2007), pp. xiii–xiv.

Responses to the Flu Epidemic of 1918

by Myra Armstead

The COVID-19 pandemic invites comparisons with a similar twentieth century worldwide plague. Just over one hundred years ago, the influenza epidemic of 1918 was a global scourge killing approximately 50 million people in a one-year period. Actually, the number of fatalities can only be estimated and range from 20 to 100 million because no one kept official records. Still, these figures are staggering. Most scholars agree there were three waves of the disease, (perhaps caused by different strains of the virus)—Spring 1918, Fall 1918, and Winter 1919—but some add a fourth that touched even previously untouched Scandinavia in 1920.[1] The first was relatively mild and limited in geographical reach, while the middle two were far more virulent and global in their deadly results. The question of origins is still a puzzle for historians of science , but almost certainly conditions in World War I activated descendants of flu strains present throughout the world from earlier, less brutal influenza pandemics in 1847 and 1889, and the outbreak may have been linked to avian flu and/or swine flu, which were unknown to scientists in 1918. The history of this pandemic allows us to reflect on public perceptions of disease, factors contributing to the spread of disease, and which populations are hardest hit by epidemics despite their undiscriminating expanse.

Overview of Progress of 1918 Flu

Contrary to what we are witnessing with the current COVID-19 pandemic, the first wave of the 1918 influenza epidemic seemed to begin in America's heartland, concentrated especially in army camps, rather than abroad and in coastal cities of the U.S. The press was relatively sluggish in picking up on the story. In late March of 1918, for instance, using federal sources, the *Grand Forks Herald* in North Dakota noted a rise in pneumonia and influenza cases, but headlined that "epidemic sicknesses are declining."[3] Similarly, the *Oregonian* announced in a most matter-of-fact way, "Mumps and influenza prevail in many National Army camps and some measles and meningitis are reported."[4] In retrospect, newspapers were relatively more concerned with an increase in cases of influenza in horses in early March.[5]

By early April, however, reports appeared of a "mysterious epidemic" affecting three hundred schoolchildren in Mexico, Missouri; thirty inmates and ten guards in the Wayne County, Michigan jail; Wayne County clerks and court attachés working in the county government building; and Ford factory workers in the Detroit area.[6] Journalists revealed that a "nuplerious malady" "hits Duluth hard," confining hundreds to their beds and crippling businesses. Although the "flurry of influenza" at Camp Custer in Battle Creek was simplistically attributed to dust, remedied by sprinkling the roads with water, authorities soon realized that the disease was spreading at an usually rapid pace and that the airborne germs carrying it could not be so easily stopped.[7] By the summer, however, new cases of the "three-day fever" dropped precipitously and the trouble seemed over in the United States.

Canada had scarcely been affected that spring. As World War I progressed, though, poor, rural Chinese workers recruited by Britain as part of the Chinese Labour Corps (non-combatants who served in France repairing damaged rails, digging trenches, unloading ships, and the like), traveled eastward across Canada to Halifax in crowded railcars on the Canadian Pacific Railway beginning in 1917. Canadian doctors dismissed the fact that 3,000 of 25,000 of the CLC employees required medical quarantine from a respiratory illness in July of 1918, and instead blamed their sickness on "Chinese laziness." Such racial stereotyping meant that many of the sick went undiagnosed, unquarantined, and traveled on to Europe where they died and the disease, already present there, spread even more swiftly in the wartime incubator.[8]

Things were hardly over in North America, though. In the Fall of 1918 and into the following winter, influenza returned with a ruthless vengeance—a byproduct of the movement of troops serving in World War I. Identified first in late August in the Boston area among sailors and soldiers docked and stationed there, the contagion quickly reached civilians. The new strain was far more vicious than the earlier one. One doctor treating patients at Camp Devens outside of Boston explained how this particular flu, starting with familiar symptoms of chills, muscle aches, and headache, progressed to a deadlier form:

> "[Victims] rapidly develop the most viscous form of Pneumonia that has ever been seen. Two hours after admission, they have the Mahogany spots over the cheek bones and a few hours later you can begin to see the Cyanosis extending from the ears and

spreading all over the face, until it is hard to distinguish the colored man from the white. It is only a matter of a few hours until death comes and it is simply a struggle for air until they suffocate. It is horrible."

On October 2 alone, the surgeon general reported 14,000 new cases within 24 hours, with a concentration in army camps like Camp Meade, Maryland; Camp Pike, Arkansas; Camp Hancock, Georgia; and Camp Funston, Kansas. By the time the pandemic ended, roughly 25 percent of Americans had suffered from the epidemic. Influenza claimed the lives of approximately 675,000 people in the United States and 50,000 in Canada— 6.5 percent and 6.1 of the total populations of those countries. Because soldiers lived in close quarters, they were highly vulnerable to the disease and contributed to the young age of those dying[10]. In stark contrast, today, the elderly are the most susceptible to COVID-19.

Then, as now, medical advice warned about the extreme contagiousness of the disease and stressed social distancing. People were warned to avoid shaking hands, to cover their mouths with masks, to remain indoors, to avoid touching library books, and not to spit in public. Large assemblies were stopped in infected army camps, and schools and theaters closed. Then as now, in the absence of a cure, scammers rushed to fill a desperate public's need by advertising and selling bogus, unscientific remedies.

Dutchess County and Our Local Women During the 1918 Flu

In Dutchess County, the *Poughkeepsie Eagle News* carried stories about a local pastor who contracted influenza while accompanying a contingent of local army volunteers by train to Camp Wheeler in Georgia and about local defiance of the order from Beacon's Commissioner of Public Safety to close all that city's saloons. There were complaints of boredom about the closing of theaters, none about the closing of churches. The paper carried appeals to county residents to join the local Red Cross in a mask-producing effort for the army camps. The newspaper also provided ostensibly expert overviews of the disease and treatments; as well as ads for questionable "Influenza Preventatives." There were, of course, many items on individuals struck by the disease—those who died and those in recovery—but admirably, there were reassuring articles reminding citizens that despite its pervasiveness, the pandemic offered "No Occasion For Panic."[11]

What of the role of the women of Dutchess County during the illness? Local women volunteered in large numbers to assist influenza victims in the emergency hospitals that were set up at the Congregational Church and City Infirmary in Poughkeepsie. The *Poughkeepsie Daily Eagle* appealed for even more hands: "Emergency Hospitals Need Women." Vassar College, all-female at the time, helped out as well. During the spring term of 1918, the junior class voted to give up its annual class trip and instead redirected those funds toward "Miss Wiley's kitchen"—a food relief service located in the quarters of the City Club for those suffering economically from the epidemic. Since so many were "feeling low in pocketbook," the Poughkeepsie City Club—a chapter of Women's City Clubs, a national social service organization—worked to address some of these problems in Dutchess County. In addition, Vassar designated a space in one of its buildings, calling it the Red Cross room, where girls also sewed nightgowns and pajamas for hospitalized victims of the "Community Calamity" described in campus posters.[12]

Conclusion

A few weeks before the 1918 pandemic gained wide notice in this country, the "Keep Well" column of the *Wilkes-Barre Times Leader*, a regular feature of that paper, offered a helpful, dispassionate, clinical description of influenza (known then also as "the grippe"):

> "Influenza may be regarded as a mild disease, the complications constituting the real danger, especially among elderly people and those who are physically 'rundown.' Of the complications the most important and dangerous are the lobar and [broncho] pneumonia. There can be no question but that there exists in all cities a certain number of carriers of the influenza germ."

Offering further historical perspective, the writer explained,

> Ancient records show that influenza epidemics were quite common. This spread always followed the lines of human travel and commerce and covers widely separated countries with such rapidity as to have produced the superstition that its onset is due to a malign 'influence;' hence its name. It is known now that there is no mysterious influence and that infection is due to [a] micro-organism.[13]

We would do well in 2020 to absorb this now 100-year old observation by practicing not only social distancing, but also mental distancing from any prejudicial, uninformed thinking on the current public health crisis.

[1] Two good articles are Niall P.A.S. Johnson and Juergen Mueller, "Updating the Accounts: Global Mortality of the 1918-1920 "Spanish" Influenza Pandemic," *Bulletin of the History of Medicine*, Vol. 76, No. 1 (Spring 2002), 105-117 and K. David Patterson and Gerald F. Pyle," The Geography and Mortality of the 1918 Influenza Pandemic," *Bulletin of the History of Medicine*, Vol. 65, No. 1 (Spring 1991), pp. 4-21. See also John M. Barry, *The Great Influenza: The Epic Story of the Deadliest Plague in History* (New York: Viking, 2004); Carol R. Byerly, *Fever of War: The Influenza Epidemic in the U.S. Army During World War I* (New York: New York University Press, 2005); Alfred W. Crosby, *America's Forgotten Pandemic: Influenza of 1918*, 2nd edition (Cambridge: Cambridge University Press, 2003); and Jeffery K. Taubenberger and David M. Morens, "1918 Influenza: The Mother of all Pandemics," *Emerging Infectious Diseases*, Vol. 12, No. 1 (January 2006), 15-22.

[2] Frequently incorrectly referred to as the 'Spanish' flu. This is because Spain, as a neutral country during WWI, left its press uncensored in its reportage on the disease, therefore contributing to a relatively high frequency of newspaper stories on influenza in that country.

[3] *Grand Forks Herald*, March 29, 1918.

[4] *The Oregonian*, March 29, 1918.

[5] *The Emporia Gazette*, March 4, 1918; The [Ann Arbor] Daily Times, March 6, 1918.

[6] *Kansas City Times*, April 3, 1918; Detroit News, April 3, 1918.

[7] *Duluth News Tribune*, April 3, 1918; Daily Times News, April 2, 1918.

[8] Mark Humphries, *The Last Plague: Spanish Influenza and the Politics of Public Health in Canada* (Toronto: University of Toronto Press, 2013), 71-72.

[9] Letter from "Roy" to a friend in Detroit, September 1918, cited in Gina Kolata, *Flu: The Story of the Great Influenza Pandemic and the Search for the Virus that Caused It* (New York: Touchstone, 2001), 13-14.

[10] *Lexington Herald*, October 2, 1918; *Macon Daily Telegraph*, October 2, 1918; *Kansas City Star*, October 2, 1918; Johnson and Mueller, "Updating the Accounts," 106, 111.

[11] *Poughkeepsie Eagle News*, October 31, 1918; *Poughkeepsie Eagle News*, October 23, 1918; Poughkeepsie Eagle News*, October 14, 1918; *Poughkeepsie Eagle News*, October 24, 1918; *Poughkeepsie Eagle News*, October 12, 1918.

[12] *Poughkeepsie Eagle-News*, October 22, 1918

[13] *Wilkes-Barre Times Leader*, March 1, 1918.

Practicing Law with Trailblazers

by Diane O'Leary

Introduction

My career in the law began in Dutchess County, New York, in 1977, not as a young woman fresh out of law school, but as a mother entering the workforce as a paralegal at age thirty-three. I worked for an established and respected attorney, Perry Satz, who had made a name for himself as the first local practitioner elected a Fellow of the American Academy of Matrimonial Lawyers. He encouraged me to become an attorney which, under his tutelage, I eventually did. With two young children at home, I pursued an unconventional path, the study of law in a law office under the Rules of the Court of Appeals.[1] Those rules permit one to sit for the bar examination after the successful completion of one year of law school followed by the study of law under an attorney for thirty-six months, a clerkship. After meeting those requirements, passing the bar examination, and satisfying the state's character committee of my moral fitness and good repute, I was admitted to practice in 1984 at age thirty-nine.

In those early paralegal years, there were but a few female practitioners in Dutchess County. I became familiar with two of them during my clerkship since Attorney Satz had many cases with them. He respected them and their work as did other members of the Bar. I looked forward to joining their ranks. While aware of their stellar reputations, I knew nothing then of their backgrounds or personal lives. Having benefited from their example, their high standards, professional and personal, and their talents, perseverance and character, I now tell their stories.

Charlotte M. Frank and Susanna E. Bedell, Women Lawyers as Trailblazers

At the onset of my career at the Bar, attorneys Charlotte M. Frank (Figure 1) and Susanna E. Bedell (Figure 2) were already in their sixties and had reached the peaks of their careers. Over time I became familiar with them both, Susanna more than Charlotte as Susanna, who outlived Charlotte by sixteen years, attended some meetings of the Mid-Hudson Women's Bar Association (a chapter of the Women's Bar Association of the State of New York " WBASNY") while I was its president for two terms (1990-1992). I eventually had cases with both as they each practiced matrimonial law as did I. Charlotte, a sole practitioner, practiced it almost exclusively and was known locally as one of our premier matrimonial attorneys.

Susanna possessed a first-class reputation as an accomplished litigator of varying issues both in the trial and appellate courts. She particularly enjoyed appellate work, which included legal research, the preparation of written briefs and, ultimately, oral argument. Matrimonial cases were among the least of her liking, as she found many of the clients too emotional.[2] Nonetheless, she handled her share expertly.

Figure 1. Charlotte M. Frank, 1981. Photograph. Dutchess County Bar Association.

Figure 2. Susanna E. Bedell, 1981. Photograph. Dutchess County Bar Association.

Charlotte was reputed to wear down her opponents to get matters resolved, indefatigably, but in a congenial way, disarmingly at times. Local opposing counsel became her friends, finding her quite proper in manner and dress. Attorney Leonard Klein fondly recalls her white gloves. Attorney Elizabeth Shequine describes her as having been incredibly intuitive. Both report that she could be counted on to extend professional courtesy, that her word could be trusted, and that her ethics were unquestioned.[3] Charlotte's clients loved her for going that extra mile for them such as the time she managed to have a father jailed for non-payment of child support, an outcome making her both feared and sought after.[4]

Susanna's litigation skills and preparedness with her no-holds-barred reputation made her formidable as well. She called them as she saw them, as the saying goes, often in good humor and sometimes using some of the more colorful words of our English language, not her native tongue. Professionally, when she used the correct word, such as to name a body part or activity, she purportedly shocked some. But never did she compromise her case, her intellectual honesty, or her unquestionable professional ethics. I saw these women as a bit intimidating, such big shoes to fill. With hindsight, I see their big shoes and broad shoulders were as much of a gift to us, the women coming after them, as a challenge.

Charlotte and Susanna, born in different countries within two years of each other, early 1917 and late 1918, respectively, are now considered in the local legal community to be pioneers, among the first to come and leaving a positive impact. Blessed with the intellect required for their chosen profession, they were fortunate to have been born of parents with education and means. Nonetheless, their privileged backgrounds did not guarantee either an easy path forward. Both faced obstacles imposed by history, culture and personal tragedy.

Susanna E. Bedell

Susanna Bedell was born Susanna Eszenyi in Budapest, Hungary on December 22, 1918 of wealthy parents. Her father was an agronomist. In her early years she lived in Budapest with her parents and younger brother in a home she later described as a "palace". The family had the luxury of a car as well as horses. Her parents separated—there being no divorce in Hungary—when she was ten. Her younger brother remained with their father. Susanna and her mother moved to her mother's family "farm" (actually a 2,000 acre plus estate with livestock and a substantial tobacco crop upon which several servant families, referred to as "peasants" in those days, lived in five *tanyas* to do the work). She described that family residence as a "castle." Susanna's destiny was eventually to inherit and run the estate so, after her early education in a convent school, she was sent to the Hungarian Royal Academy of Agriculture.

Susanna's mother, Rosemarie (who everyone called "Zsoka"), a significant influence in her life, was well-educated. She was a member of a chamber music group and read Dante in Italian for pleasure. Eventually living with a man ten years her junior, Zsoka was ahead of her time in many ways. She managed the business of the estate, set up a school for the servants' children and, contrary to the Catholic Church's teachings, was so distressed over how producing child after child destroyed their health, she advised the mothers about birth control and dispensed contraceptives.

Figure 3. Susanna E. Bedell as a young woman (Susanna Eszenyi), c.1940. Photograph. Collection of Dr. Susanna Bedell.

By age seventeen, Susanna knew that her future was not secure. As she described it: "First we had the War and then we had the Germans, and then we had the Russians and the Russians were real bad news for people of wealth and stature." Determined to go to the United States, Susanna took matters into her own hands. She left Hungary in 1938 (never to return until a reunion at her convent school in 1996). She obtained a scholarship to Vassar College for one year, entering as a junior to major in Botany, a scholarship she managed to extend. While at Vassar, and in the fall of 1939, she learned that her brother, back in Hungary and living with their father, had died tragically at age seventeen.

A few months later, and in the spring of 1940, Susanna finished her college education (Figure 3). After graduation, she obtained research work in cytology at Columbia University, finding the research important but "dreary." She took an aptitude test offered by Stevens Institute in New Jersey: it suggested a career in the law. Susanna managed to gain entry into Columbia University's law school, joining a class of "boys" and "girls" as she called them, 150 "boys" and 10 "girls", with the class of "boys" shrinking considerably beginning in 1942 as they went off to war following Pearl Harbor.

Continually struggling to learn English and understand American culture, Susanna obtained additional scholarships as her family was stripped of its wealth. She lost all contact with her parents. Her beloved mother died in 1944, a fact unknown to her until a year later. She learned that her father was taken by the Russians and never seen or heard from again. She presumed her grandparents were dead and she had no knowledge of how, when, or where anyone was buried. There was no immediate family left. Her native country, Hungary, was at war with the United States. A back injury in 1942 (which Susanna then attributed to lifting laundry and later admitted was at least partially psychological), landed her in a nursing home for four months, leaving her unable to graduate with the classmates with whom she had begun. She graduated in 1944 alone in a new country at age twenty-six, embarking on a demanding career while she was, officially, an enemy alien.

After graduation, Susanna received seven offers from eight "white-shoe" law firms to which she had applied. She did not get an interview with the well-known White & Case law firm as the firm did not then interview women. She took a position at the equally prestigious firm of Sherman & Sterling in New York City where she worked from 1944-1951. In the beginning, she was sent to meetings of the firm's corporate clients and other assignments visibly representing the firm as its men were still off to war. When they returned, she was relegated to the in-house legal research pool (which likely honed her excellent research skills).

Securely on her way to a significant career, Susanna became engaged to a young man she later described as a member of the New York Upper 400, "a miserable lot!" The engagement was brief. She broke it off, unable to abide his complaining about such things as being tired at the end of the day from such tasks as picking out suits for himself while she was busy working. Not long after, in 1947, she married Wallace Bedell ("Wally"), a young man she had met while at Vassar. Wally was embarking on a medical career as she continued at Sherman & Sterling. With the onset of the Korean War, her husband's military assignment to the Naval Hospital at Bethesda brought them to the Washington D.C. area. While there, Susanna obtained a position at the prestigious firm of Wilmer & Broun, handling its First Amendment cases. In about 1955, when Wally's military commitment ended, the couple and their two children settled in Pough-keepsie where he established his career as a surgeon.

Susanna opened her own law practice in Poughkeepsie. Discouraged that she earned only $900 the first year, she concluded that the combination of being a female attorney, a foreigner and not a Poughkeepsie native were obstacles she could not overcome at that time. So, at age thirty-eight, Susanna spent the next ten years out of the practice of law, continuing to raise their two children, Susanna and Wallace (then affectionately called "Bambi" and "Joey") and offering her skills to her new community, making valuable connections and long term friendships while serving on several boards and organizations (for a while seven at one time), including the League of Women Voters and the W.W. Smith Center.

In 1967 Susanna suffered a deep and bitter disappointment, the end of her marriage, yet another personal loss. She found herself, at age forty-eight, having to earn a living. She reentered the legal profession, at first working for the Aldrich brothers, and then becoming Of Counsel to the law firm of Van DeWater& Van DeWater where she found a home in which to practice law for the remainder of her career. She passed away on October 11, 2006 at age eighty-seven.

Charlotte M. Frank

Charlotte Frank, a contemporary of Susanna Bedell, also enjoyed a privileged background. Charlotte was born January 28, 1917 in Poughkeepsie into an Irish Roman Catholic family, the daughter of Dr. James E. McCambridge and Isabelle Milford McCambridge. During her early years, the family lived in a townhouse on Mill Street. Her father and his brother, also a physician, were instrumental in the building of St. Francis Hospital as, being Catholic, they could not obtain privileges at Vassar Hospital. Charlotte attended Putnam Hall School in Poughkeepsie in her early years, boarded at Marymount School for some of her high school years, then finished at Oakwood Friends School. She attended Vassar College for a time, then transferred to Earlham College in Indiana, a Quaker institution, graduating in 1940. After further education at the University of Michigan, she attended St. John's University School of Law, graduated in 1945, and was admitted to the Bar in due course.

Like Susanna, Charlotte had one sibling, a brother. In those days when so much emphasis was put on a son's education, one might wonder what would drive a girl like Charlotte to higher education and a profession. In addition to a culture of high achievement in her father's family among the men, her mother Isabelle (purportedly related to the Smith Brothers), who only went to the sixth grade, counseled Charlotte from an early age that she must achieve a good education so as to never have to rely on a husband, not the usual advice from a mother in those days. In addition to a traditional education, Isabelle sent Charlotte to a camp each summer

Figure 4. Charlotte M. Frank, 1948. Photograph. Dutchess County Bar Association.

which emphasized survival skills and team building. Charlotte went from camper to counselor over her formative years. No one could have predicted the course Charlotte's life would take, but it turned out that Isabelle was prescient.

Charlotte met her future husband, Hugh Frank, in law school and married shortly thereafter. Their marriage was not acceptable to Hugh's Jewish family as he not only married outside of his faith but converted to Catholicism. After law school, Charlotte obtained a position as a law secretary to a judge (a position held by an attorney to assist the judge with legal research, writing opinions and sometimes holding conferences with the opposing attorneys on a case to attempt to settle it). She told her children that in those days male law school graduates generally got those plum positions in the Courts while female graduates often settled for clerical work, so when she interviewed for the position she stated, in no uncertain terms, "I DO NOT TYPE." In 1948, Charlotte and Hugh opened a private law practice together in Poughkeepsie, the law firm of Frank and Frank (Figure 4). Charlotte envisioned that Hugh would devote his full time to the practice and she would practice part time while raising their three children, Christine, William and James ("Chris," "Billy," and "Jimmy").

Chris Krok, the oldest, recalls that when her mother was pregnant, she was not about to let it interfere with her career. Charlotte traveled to New York City to the Tailored Woman at Fifth Avenue and 57th Street, to have clothes custom made for her to hide her pregnancies, believing that no one would hire her knowing she was pregnant, a masquerade that apparently worked. The couple's practice seemingly got off to a good start as Charlotte found the time to engage in local and State Bar activities, including becoming a member of the Executive Committee of the Young Lawyers Section of the New York State Bar Association and hosting an event in Poughkeepsie in 1954. However, Charlotte's life upended in about 1958 when she was forty-one years old.

When Chris was in the sixth grade, she remembers that her father, Hugh Frank, disappeared from their lives, never to return to the family or support them in any way. Charlotte's mother had died by then, and her father was retired and getting on in years. Charlotte could not and did not skip a beat. Her survival mentality kicked in. While maintaining her Poughkeepsie office, she moved the family, including her father, to Pine Plains in 1959 to expand her practice and provide a healthy, country atmosphere for her three children. She wanted what her mother Isabelle wanted for her, well-rounded, self-sufficient children. She faced having to accomplish that alone.

Her daughter Chris recalls that Charlotte would work all day in Pough-keepsie, come home and change out of her" lawyer clothes" into something comfortable, have dinner with them, then change back and see clients in her home office in the evening. While Charlotte hired housekeepers, she also made sure the children shared the domestic chores, like getting dinner and cleaning up. Chris recalls that Charlotte would not install the dish-washer Grandpa bought for her early on because she believed that doing dishes as a team brought the family together for conversation at the end of the day. Chris noted, wistfully, that when Charlotte died in 1990, over thirty years later, that dishwasher was still in the garage.

The children helped with the law practice, answering the door to greet clients and, when they were old enough, they even served legal process for her. Imagine a cute, curly-haired young woman armed with a Summons and Complaint for a divorce, catching an unsuspecting spouse off guard, particularly one trying to avoid service of those dreaded documents!

Memories

With determination and hard work, Charlotte managed to send all three children to the best private schools, camps and institutes of higher learning. Chris became a special education teacher, Billy and Jimmy both became doctors. Susanna, like Charlotte, also produced well-educated children who have made their own marks in life. Her daughter Susanna became a doctor and her son, an architect. Susanna's and Charlotte's daughters speak poignantly of the mothers they so much admired, dearly loved and miss. (Dr.) Susanna Bedell recounts how she relished those after-school moments sitting at the kitchen table having cookies and milk with her mother with whom she knew she could talk about anything. Chris Krok cherishes the memory of the periodic trips she and her brothers took with their mother, such as to Mount Greylock in the Berkshire Mountains, embarking in the wee hours of the morning to catch the sunrise and cook breakfast over an open fire at the summit. Both mothers found rejuvenation in nature. Charlotte purchased a cabin at nearby Stissing Lake for seclusion and privacy, finding peace drifting in her canoe. Susanna found refuge "grubbing" in her expansive gardens, forever the botanist.

Giving Back

With all they faced, both women not only managed to command respect as competent attorneys and raise successful children, they each volunteered time to their profession. For many years, on behalf of the State,

Susanna conducted those mandatory interviews that all candidates for admission to the Bar endure to pass the character and fitness requirement, an appointment only offered to those deemed of exemplary character and fitness themselves. Attorney Phillip Shatz, in his tribute to Susanna after her death remarked about those interviews that, "No young lawyer ever forgot that event and substantially all of them became her friends." My daughter, Attorney Sharon Faulkner, recalls her 2001 interview with Susanna with a chuckle. When Susanna saw that Sharon was previously admitted in Hawaii and practiced on Maui for over ten years, she quipped that she was not so sure she could find Sharon "fit" for leaving paradise to practice in New York!

Charlotte Frank made her mark as a true pioneer and trailblazing woman in 1982 in becoming the first woman president of the Dutchess County Bar Association. This ground-breaking achievement was even more significant as she was a sole practitioner paid for her time by the hour, making it difficult to engage in time-consuming volunteer activities without the underlying support of a firm. After her years of service to our county bar, she continued to work tirelessly for her clients to the end. In fact, it was on her way driving from her home in Pine Plains to her Poughkeepsie office in 1990 that she suffered a stroke which was to take her soon after at the all too young age of seventy-three.

Gratitude

Charlotte and Susanna achieved success while confronting the challenges imposed by the culture of their time. There was the obvious challenge of gaining acceptance in a profession historically dominated by men. Not so obvious was the challenge of being accepted by the women who worked for years in the legal community in roles subordinate to the men. During my early years in the law so many women, legal secretaries, would say to me that they could NEVER work for a woman! Then there was the matrimonial practice itself, one saturated with clients in crisis, with no matter more devastating than a child custody battle.

Perhaps because of her own circumstances, Charlotte demonstrated a lot of empathy. Her support not only inured to the benefit of her clients, but to her female staff and colleagues as well. She understood the challenges other women faced. A secretary in my law firm, Shiela Ryder, worked for Charlotte in the past for several years. Over Shiela's many years with us, she often spoke of Charlotte with gratitude, an employer who understood the pressures of a working mother. It was okay to leave early to care for a sick child. One of Charlotte's early and longtime friends was a secretary in the Family Court. Charlotte befriended a kindred spirit, a woman in a male-dominated workplace seeking to gain confidence and the respect of the men. It has been many years since I last heard any woman say she would never work for a woman, in fact, quite the contrary.

Susanna understood the rigors of the practice of law, particularly matrimonial law, and was eager to offer advice to her colleagues. Back in the early '90s at the Family Court, as Susanna and I waited for our respective cases to be called, we commiserated over the emotional and physical toll the practice took on our bodies and minds. Susanna, who promoted the value of eating a healthy diet and used regular swimming and yoga practice to deal with stress, asked for my home address. Within a week, an article arrived in my mail on the benefit of eating celery to alleviate hypertension and anxiety. A reformed smoker, Susanna spoke of the dangers of tobacco to whomever would listen, even enrolling a young colleague, Kathryn Lazar, in a class to help her kick the habit, such an irony as Susanna's original destiny was to run a huge tobacco enterprise in Hungary.

These women not only inspired us, they supported us. Consider this final recollection provided by Kathryn Lazar, taken under Susanna's wing when Kathryn was a new lawyer: The setting was a Dutchess County Bar Association lunch meeting at the Amrita Club in the late '70s, a time when women, among other groups, were not welcome as club members. The attendees were all men except for no more than five women, attorneys, Susanna and Kathryn among them. All seated, the speaker, an attorney from Westchester County, began his presentation with the greeting "GENTLEMEN:" whereupon Susanna stood up and inquired, "Sir, are you planning on addressing the entire audience?" When Kathryn later commented to Susanna, "You need not have done that, it's fine", Susanna disagreed, stating, "I did that for you."

A Last Word

Susanna Bedell and Charlotte Frank, as trailblazers, set a high bar for us, the women attorneys who followed, while making that bar easier to reach. We all benefited, particularly those of us who litigated. I believe that we approached the bench for the first time perhaps enjoying a little more respect than we might have otherwise because of the respect they earned before us.

[1] Section 520.4 Study of Law in Law Office, of Part 520. Rules of the Court of Appeals for the Admission of Attorneys and Counselors at Law, *McKinney's New York Rules of Court Volume1-State2020* (Thomson Reuters 2019). I would like to thank the families and friends of Charlotte Frank and Susanna Bedell for sharing their time and memories, especially Chris Krok, Dr. Susanna Bedell, and Kathryn Lazar. I am also grateful to Janna Whearty of the Dutchess County Bar Association for her generous assistance.

[2] Except as otherwise indicated in this text, the information provided concerning the background of Susanna E. Bedell is from the following documents: A transcript, as revised on April 4, 1998, of *Interview for Oral History Project on The Women at Columbia Law School* between Evan A. Davis and Susanna E. Bedell conducted at Poughkeepsie, New York on May 4, 1997 at 3:00 p.m. and an essay by Susanna E. Bedell titled *Four Generations of Women* sent to Edith S. Lessor, Hudson Valley OWL, on January 24, 1997. The direct quotations are from the oral history. Both documents are the property of Kathryn S. Lazar.

[3] Interviews with Attorneys Elizabeth K. Shequine and Leonard Klein conducted in December 2019 and January 2020.

[4] Except as otherwise indicated in this text, the information concerning the background of Charlotte M. Frank, her thoughts and direct quotations, was provided by Christine Krok during interviews conducted in January and February 2020.

[5] Article appearing in the *New York State Bar Bulletin*, June 1954, under subtitles "Young Lawyers Elect New Officers" and "Young Lawyers Meet at Poughkeepsie," pp. 120-122, a copy provided by the Dutchess County Bar Association from its archives.

[6] Phillip Shatz, "In Memoriam Susanna Bedell, Esq.," in *The Advocate*, Winter 2006, p. 10, a publication of the Dutchess County Bar Association provided by such Association from its archives.

[7] Interview with Attorney Sharon M. Faulkner conducted in February 2020.

[8] Shiela Ryder in conversation with the author on various occasions over the years.

[9] From transcript of 1998 Interview for *Oral History Project on The women at Columbia Law School*.

[10] Ibid.

Ecology Pioneer at Vassar College

by Barbara Hughey

In 1919, a young botany professor was hired on to teach at Vassar College. Edith Adelaide Roberts was born in 1881 to a New Hampshire farming family. She had earned her doctorate at the University of Chicago under Professor Henry C. Cowles, a friend and associate of Danish landscape architect Jens Jensen. Cowles and Jensen were experts in the design of natural plantings that mimicked the mid-west prairie of the Great Plains. Dr. Roberts, in coming back east to Vassar, was able to transpose and adapt that design sensibility to Dutchess County. Her dedication and encyclopedic knowledge in the art and science of plant ecology reverberates in the fields of ecology and landscape design even today—in the current atmosphere of environmental awareness.

Figure 1. Dr. Edith A. Roberts in her office at Vassar College, n.d. Photograph. Vassar College Special Collections, Vassar College, Poughkeepsie, NY.

Having grown up on a farm, Dr. Roberts had a deep personal experience of the natural plant communities of the hedgerow, meadow, and orchard environments of the Northeast. She quickly observed that in Dutchess county agriculture, timber harvest and other disturbances had eliminated most of the pre-colonial natural habitats and she sought to recreate those environments for as a teaching tool on the Vassar campus. This took the form of a four acre native plant garden that incorporated an impressive 675 species.

With the help of her students, Dr. Roberts gathered samples of native plant species and arranged them in the garden in groupings of naturally occurring plant associations, as they would have been found in nature. She and her students worked to understand how to grow native plants from seed, which often required specialized handling to be successful. When she got word that a piece of land with desirable species was to be disturbed or developed she would organize a work force and go to rescue the plants there for the native garden or to gather the seed to stock the experimental seed bank. It was a labor of love that she spent many years of intense work pursuing. When the funds for the endeavor ran short of her goals she lectured off campus and put the money earned into her projects out of her own pocket. The resulting garden, placed near Skinner Building on the campus, was known as the Dutchess County Outdoor Ecological Laboratory. It was the first such extensive native plant garden in the country.[1]

It is interesting to note that this was underway over fifty years before Lady Bird Johnson and Helen Hayes famously founded the National Wildflower Research Center at the University of Texas. It was also before I, as a young plant and soil science student, was attending nascent versions of ecology lectures at Cornell.

Dr. Roberts intended that her students, colleagues and associates be able to experience the wide array of native plant habitats that had been in place before the county's extraordinary agricultural potential had been realized and before the ancient timber had been cut. Her work from that time has provided a foundation for what is now a widely accepted appreciation for the significance of native plants as the essential living foundation for healthy ecosystems and clean water. She advanced the study of botany and set that discipline in the context of plant ecology. She even changed the name of the Botany Department to the Department of Plant Science to reflect that scientific and ecological perspective.

In 1927, Dr. Roberts wrote a series of plant ecology articles with her colleague landscape architect Elsa Rehmann. This work was published in the popular magazine *House Beautiful*. This brought the subject of planting and protecting our beautiful native plants beyond the science curriculum at Vassar and into the hearts and minds of the average person interested in gardening and landscaping at their own homes. In 1929, these same articles were compiled and reprinted as the chapters for a highly regarded book called *American Plants for American Gardens*.[2] Of course 1929 was also the year of the financial collapse of the Great Depression that changed our world in so many important ways. One of those was to do with the shift in how and where landscapes were designed. Both public works and private estate garden installations ceased to be affordable. The enthusiasm for natural design gradually fell away and was replaced by an aesthetic more concerned with geometric shape and a spare structural character. This approach known as the Modern Era of landscape design made use of fewer species and large tracts of turf. Collecting and using exotic specimen plants from around the world became the thing to have. Status was assigned to the rare and hard to find and native plants were derisively labeled weeds.

Those of us who are interested in the environmental sciences now understand that it is actually the escaped exotic plants from agriculture and

Figure 2. Bench in restored wetland with alders, 2014. Photograph. Vassar College, Poughkeepsie, NY. Collection of Karl Rabe.

horticulture that have become invasive weedy species. These imported plants threaten, by over competition and other noxious effects, our regionally adapted native flora.

Dr. Roberts taught at Vassar College from 1918 until 1948. Her life's work as a dedicated educator and scientific pioneer continues to provide us with the informational tools to shift the way we interact with our landscapes from decorative plant collectors to land stewards.

Every environmental, wildlife, and botanical conservation organization in the world now states unequivocally that encouraging and planting native plants is an essential part of renewing the quality and character of our landscapes big and small. We have Native Plant centers, nurseries, clubs and organizations. This knowledge has also led to the creation of invasive species councils. Here in New York State there are seven regional Partnerships for Invasive Species Management. There are huge, ever expanding budgets for invasive species controls that exceed a hundred billion dollars per year in the U.S., all to regain the native plant habitats that we have allowed to dwindle.

In 1996, *American Plants for American Gardens* was reissued with the help of and with a forward by world renowned landscape architect Darrel G. Morrison.[3] The scope of understanding in the fields of horticulture and ecology has evolved in ways that were perhaps unimagined in the 1920s but Dr. Roberts' contribution is still influential today. Morrison, whose work is centered on sustainable design and the importance of conveying a sense of place in landscape, credits her with greatly influencing his work. He has related that in the early part of his career he was following the

Figure 3. Wet meadow plants; Joe Pye weed in bloom (Eupatorium sp.). 2014. Photograph. Vassar College, Poughkeepsie, NY. Collection of Karl Rabe.

generic traditions in landscaping that were common during his training in the 1960s, but that he "saw the light" when he read Edith Roberts and Elsa Rehmann's book which influenced him to refocus his work on the creation of naturalized plantings.

Mr. Morrison's truly remarkable work in our region has reached countless numbers of people through the public spaces he has so expertly created.[4] These include the Native Plant Extension at the Brooklyn Botanical Garden. This glorious garden focuses our attention on communities of plant species found within a two hundred mile radius of New York City. It shows off to great benefit the beauty of combining ecologically appropriate plants in naturalized drifts with year round aesthetic value. Mr. Morrison is also responsible for the majestic meadow themed plantings at the Storm King Sculpture Park. These grass and wild flower expanses perfectly set off the large scale sculpture there. Dr. Roberts' design philosophy and tradition reaches a new group of nature inspired designers through Mr. Morrison's students at Columbia University. He has said that he strives to instill the importance of getting out in natural environments, to experience and assimilate the lessons of nature as the best teacher for responsible landscape architectural design.

Chapter by chapter, the major ecological habitats of our region were described in *America Plants for American Gardens* beautifully and in great detail. What is conveyed is an appreciation for the importance of place, but also the absolute worthiness of these wild plant species for achieving aesthetic excellence in the curated landscape.

When Dr. Roberts and Dr. Rehmann chose to work together, a cross disciplinary synergy was achieved that gave us both the scientific Latin plant names for the eleven habitats described with easy to execute recommendations for their use.

Every chapter in the book was followed by a list of plants found in each environmental category. In all there are 2000 plants named. Among the chapter headings are: the juniper hillside, the gray birches, the hemlock ravine, the stream side, and others.

The authors introduce the ways in which each phase of plant community occupation of a particular site in the introduction of American Plants for American Gardens.

> One plant group is no sooner established than its very development changes the light, the temperature and the moisture

conditions to such a degree that a new group comes in and succeeds the first. The definiteness of these transitions is shown by the way the junipers, gray birches, the pines, the oaks and the maple, beech or hemlock follow one another in succession. On the uplands the fields are filled with sun-loving herbs and shrubs. They make a congenial place for the germination of juniper seeds. The shade and protection of the junipers encourages the development of the seed of the birches. Birch copses in their turn are nurseries for the pines. The pine green, too dense for its own seed, provides the right conditions for the oaks. In their maturity the oaks make an excellent environment for the development of the maple, beech and hemlocks. All three of these spring up within their own shade, but where the shade becomes deepest and where it is coolest the hemlocks dominate.[5]

The process of plant community succession is nestled into the work such that we can almost learn it by osmosis. The contextual framework of plant name identified place, and how it came to be is revealed. The *"Open Field"* is a result of disturbance of some kind in what was a forest dominated landscape, such as fire, or something man made, such as agricultural clearing and tilling. If left to its own devises, it would evolve naturally into a shrub land with dogwoods and junipers taking hold. That the conditions created by one successional association adjusted the growing conditions such that the way is paved for a stepwise progression back to climax forest. Every stage of the process over time is completely connected to the changes in light, moisture and soil conditions that each successive wave of colonizers imparts.

This message was crafted to provide a guide for becoming beneficial collaborators with nature as we plan our own gardens and landscapes. As designers we can reset the successional clock and encourage the best use of a particular habitat. It teaches us to look for our inspiration from the natural areas that we are so fortunate to still have around us. It also incorporates that inspiration with a call to action. The chapter entitled *The Juniper Hillside* includes this message:

Unfortunately, in the course of time and circumstance, the plow may have uprooted many of the shrubs and flowers, and the ax cut away the trees. If that is so, there is a marvelous incentive to recreate what has been destroyed. And if all the plants of particular hillside have been cleared away, other exiting examples can become inspiring guides for their reproduction.[6]

Figure 4. Dr. Meg Ronsheim, professor of Plant Science at Vassar College. Dr. Ronsheim with two students removing invasive species roots. 2014. Photograph. Vassar College, Poughkeepsie, NY. Collection of Karl Rabe.

In another section—in the chapter *The Gray Birches*, the authors use a more poetic method when they write:

> Wherever there are gray birches, Nature is in one of her lightest moods. These gray trees of slender form gather together in fairy-like groves. Their slim grace is accentuated by the way they often spring up in fives and sixes from a single root. When they are young they are gray brown but later on they are phantom white with black twigs and black notches. The effect is full of that mystery that etchings and delicate pencil drawings have.[7]

As an environmentally focused plant professional, I am amazed that horticultural and agricultural practices are still in the process of catching up with the critical importance of recognizing the beauty and intelligence of using nature as our principal teacher for how to interact with our rich and precious environment. Fashion and expedience are poor replacements for that guidance.

These days there is a new generation of science students at Vassar College that is engaged with the restoration of the Vassar Ecological Research

Laboratory under the supervision of Dr. Meg Ronsheim, professor of plant science. Dr. Ronsheim discovered the all but abandoned historic garden of Dr. Edith Roberts in the early 1990s, and was able to appreciate that the wild array of unusual plants that were in place there had in fact been planted by someone. She started to investigate the back story of the garden and realized that this was something to protect and nurture.[8]

In July 2013, *The New York Times* published an article detailing the renewed interest and investment in Dr. Edith Roberts' Native Plant Garden.[9] This restoration is both historical and environmental. In a phone interview with Meg Ronsheim, she expressed her deep appreciation to Dr. Roberts as a pioneering woman of science and dedicated educator.[10] Today, Dr. Ronsheim continues the tradition of teaching people to see what the healthy plant communities look like, and how it feels to be among them. She is working to introduce to her students is a completely consistent theme inherited from Dr. Roberts' own philosophy. This is what was handed down through Dr. Edith Roberts' students, through Mr. Darrel Morrison's work, through his students, and now to Dr. Ronsheim and her new groups of twenty-first century students. It is an immensely active and hopeful lineage.

---

[1]   See Lance Ringel, "Edith Roberts: A Haven for Native Plants," *Vassar Alumnae Quarterly* (V. 108, Issue 3, Fall, 2012). Edith A. Roberts, and Helen Wilkinson Reynolds. *"The Role of Plant Life in the History of Dutchess County."* (Copyrighted by authors 1938).

[2]   Edith A. Roberts and Elsa Rehmann. *American Plants for American Gardens.* (Macmillan Company, 1929. Athens and London: The University of Georgia Press, 1996).

[3]   Ibid.

[4]   Darrel Morrison, *The Landscape is Our Teacher.* You Tube, Uploaded by Round House Wilton, December 3, 2017.

[5]   Edith A. Roberts and Elsa Rehmann, Ibid., Introduction.

[6]   Ibid., "The Juniper Hillside" chapter.

[7]   Ibid., "The Gray Birches" chapter.

[8]   Meg Ronsheim, Interview with Barbara Hughey. January 21, 2020.

[9] Lisa W. Foderaro, "Vassar Revives Garden Nurtured by Early Promoter of Native Plants." *New York Times* (July 25, 2013).

[10] Meg Ronsheim, Interview with Barbara Hughey. Ibid. See also Lance Ringel, "Edith Roberts: A Haven for Native Plants," *Vassar Alumnae Quarterly* (V. 108, Issue 3, Fall, 2012).

"I'll be right over"

by Meg Downey

Blunt and at times acerbic, she was also quick to laugh, a distinctive throaty chuckle. Dr. Josephine Evarts lived by the mantra "I'll be right over." She loved children and animals, and like a fierce archangel, fumed over the stupidity of the human race. The no-nonsense "Dr. Jo," in more than 50 years as a physician, helped thousands of people in New York's Harlem Valley and northwestern Connecticut. As a country doctor, Evarts, treated "whatever comes in," which was mostly bruised souls. "If they fall downstairs and get a black and blue mark, they want you to look at it," she said. "I don't have a very healing look, but I never refuse to see someone. They like to feel somebody loves them, that they have someone to lean on."

Figure 1. Dr. Josephine Evarts at her Millerton office late in her career. Photograph. Bob Kristofik, Poughkeepsie Journal.

Evarts, who died in 1983 at age 81, did whatever needed to be done to serve—whether it meant getting down on the floor to deliver a baby, defying state bureaucrats to protect mentally ill patients, or milking a cow on behalf of a hospitalized farmer. "You need a lot of energy," she said in a 1979 interview about her career. "You must be interested in the patient's point of view and be willing to listen. A certain amount of kindliness is a good idea."[1]

And a certain amount of objectivity.

"A doctor must be able to get out of bed at night and sign a death certificate and get back in again," she said. "You can't spend too much time fussing over the inevitable." She relied on nature and common sense and a sturdy New England upbringing that valued books, good conversation, a spiritual center rooted in Biblical verse and a can-do attitude. And she did listen. Her eyes would never leave your face. And if you did or said something foolish, the look could be withering. "I don't love mankind," she once told the Poughkeepsie Journal, "and I think people act so stupid sometimes. I don't even know if mankind is worth saving. But I think people are funny, and I like to be useful. So here I am."[2]

Dr. Jo's Family History

Born in Windsor, Vermont, on Aug. 16, 1901, Josephine was the youngest of five children of Maxwell and Margaret Stetson Evarts, both from New York City. Her father, a graduate of Yale and then Harvard Law School like his father before him, served as general counsel for the Union Pacific Railroad. He had been hired by railroad baron E. H. Harriman, father of W. Averell Harriman, who later would become governor of New York. Her father spent weekdays in New York or Washington, often arguing before the U.S. Supreme Court defending the railroad in antitrust cases. He commuted to Vermont on the weekends where he then oversaw the family farm and estate as well as the local bank he founded and other local businesses he invested in. Jo's work ethic appeared to be genetic.

Her grandfather, attorney William Maxwell Evarts, successfully defended President Andrew Johnson in his impeachment trial in 1868 and would later serve as U.S. Attorney General under Johnson, U.S. Secretary of State under Hayes and Garfield and then U.S. Senator from New York. (Dr. Jo hung a Thomas Nast cartoon lambasting her grandfather in her guest bathroom.) A great-great grandfather, Roger Sherman of Connecticut, signed the Declaration of Independence.

Jo's father was one of 12 children so she had numerous cousins. One of her first cousins she was fond of was Maxwell Perkins, the famed book editor who discovered Ernest Hemingway and F. Scott Fitzgerald. Perkin's sister, Jo's cousin Frances, was the mother of Archibald Cox Jr., special prosecutor during the Watergate scandal. During the televised hearings of the Senate Watergate Committee in 1973, Jo would spend her lunch hour at home riveted to the TV set.

Late in her life, at a dinner where she was being honored for a lifetime of serving others, Josephine Evarts acknowledged her remarkable background. "I think," she told the audience who had given her a standing ovation, "what you are all really interested in and grateful for is a way of life which was the result of an extraordinary upbringing in the state of Vermont in a household with two remarkable parents who knew enough to have children and love them and let them be."[3]

Dr. Jo's Childhood and Education

Jo and her siblings were schooled at home in the morning by tutors and then given the afternoons to play on the farm, roam the woods and do their chores, mostly caring for the farm animals. Jo claimed to have learned pediatrics by tending to disowned piglets. Feeding chickens and sheep, milking cows, chopping wood, breaking her family's treasured Morgan colts, she reveled in it. And in the evenings, poetry was recited, and her mother read or recited the Scriptures to her at night before she went to bed.

At 15, Jo left home to attend Miss Porter's School for girls in Farmington, Conn., and graduated in 1920. She then went to Vassar College in Pough-keepsie, where she graduated in 1924. She had often gone riding and had talks with Prexy, Vassar's renowned president Henry Noble MacCracken. At Vassar, a speech by a missionary working with sick refugees turned her to medicine.

"As a child," she said, "I was not sure whether I wanted to be a veterinarian or a detective, and I think it was not until I was a freshman in college that I decided—if I studied medicine I could sort of combine the two, and it made me feel needed."[4]

Evarts was one of 12 women in a medical school class of 100 at the Columbia University College of Physicians and Surgeons in New York City. Harvard wasn't taking women then, though Johns Hopkins did. "However," she said, "I usually take the line of least resistance. I didn't have to take calculus to get into P&S."[5] She spoke of how male medical students would sabotage the laboratory experiments of their female classmates. She just did the experiments over.

Dr. Jo's Practice

Dr. Jo worked as an intern with no pay at Bellevue Hospital in New York and then "hung out her shingle" in 1929 in Cornwall, Conn., just as the Great Depression hit. She saw its effects. She helped deliver at home the seventh child of a family living in an abandoned henhouse. "They made $30 a month," she said, "and had one quart of milk a day, which was promptly consumed by whoever was the youngest baby. At the home delivery, every time I tried to sit down on a chair to rest my bones, I found I was sitting on a small child." She found jobs for the father whenever she heard of someone who needed a hired hand, until finally the family was making $65 a month and had all of the milk they needed. Years later, when she could no longer remember their names, she was traveling through a small Connecticut town and saw a road crew. "One of them hailed me," she said. "I stopped, and he waved a roll of bills at me and said, 'I've been carrying this money around for a long time, and this is the first time I've seen you. You know you never sent me a bill.' "It would have insulted him, but I hadn't wanted to waste the postage—I accepted the money and went on my way."[6]

Evarts did for her patients whatever had to be done. She answered calls at all hours, pulled teeth, brought them food in a child's wagon that she would pull behind her, and drove people to the hospital when needed. In one case, a farmer suffering from acute appendicitis was reluctant to get in her car to go to the hospital because his wife and farm hand could not properly care for the animals. She ordered him into the car and promised to take care of the animals. Until he recovered, she fed the pigs and milked the cow daily by hand.

Jo used folk remedies as much as modern medications. Her prescriptions for healing included eating raw onions to relieve head colds, using meat tenderizer mixed with spit to counter bee stings, and applying honey to cuts as an antiseptic. A little whiskey could help diminish a fever, including for children. But she valued modern medications and kept up with the latest research. She was a member of the New York Academy of Medicine and member and past president of the Litchfield County Medical Society, the oldest in the United States.

Jo often found what others missed. She ordered a glucose tolerance test for a patient who persistently felt faint. For years this patient's doctors had not recognized hypoglycemia. Dr. William Herrick, past president of the New York Academy of Medicine, called Jo "one of the most brilliant diagnosticians that I've ever worked with." And if she saw a need, she filled it. She learned how to practice anesthesiology at Sharon Hospital because someone had to do it. But she never wanted to specialize because she considered it dull to do the same thing every day.

Jo was as much a psychologist as a general practitioner and knew how to use human nature as one of her aids. She had a patient with stomach ulcers whom she told to eat a spice-free diet and avoid coffee and alcohol. The pain went away and the patient asked if he should have a test to see if the ulcers were gone. "I don't recommend it," Jo responded. "If the new tests show that they haven't entirely cleared up, you'll continue to be careful but you'll worry knowing you still have them. If the new tests show no sign of ulcers, you're apt to celebrate and get careless about your diet, and the ulcers are likely to return. Why not continue avoiding coffee, alcohol, spicy food, doctors, hospitals, and tests?"[7]

For all of her generosity, she could be cranky, abrupt, judgmental, and infuriating. One of her colleagues, Dr. Carnes Weeks, recalled that after filling in for her while she was on vacation, he heard, upon her return, a litany of criticism about how he handled her patients on top of his own. Just when he was ready to explode, she'd put her arm around him and tell some off-color joke. He then could not help but laugh, she would be forgiven, and the world would right itself again.[8]

Bill Crawford, a former ambulance driver from Millerton, remembers having to drive a patient down to a New York City hospital that he had not been to before. "So Dr. Jo was giving me directions on how to get there," he said. "When she was finished, I asked her to go over it again. I didn't want to get lost. She said, 'I told you once. What are you, stupid?' Luckily, I had remembered it correctly."

Marion Snyder recalled how sometime around 1966 Dr. Evarts came to her house and "while sitting there listening to her advice, my son— about 5—was trying to get my attention by hitting my arm, 'Mom, Mom,' when Dr. Evarts grabbed him, put him over her knee and gave him a few good "swats." She said, "A boy who hits his mother will grow up to hit his wife." He ran to his room, and she just continued to give me her wisdom. Shocked into silence, I sure never forgot that day. Before she left, she went to his door and said some comforting words. That boy didn't grow up to hit his wife—or anyone else."

Jo was particularly tough on those she felt were deliberating harming themselves. Ellie Lowell of Millerton remembers, as a child, that her father had gone to the emergency room for a head injury and "Doc came out to find Mom, and she was outside smoking. She said the cigs would kill her way before a few stitches in his noggin would."

Dr. Evarts had no problem bucking authority. And she did not hesitate to use unorthodox methods of treatment when warranted. When she worked at Harlem Valley State Hospital in Wingdale from 1968 to 1971, she took her German shepherd Diamond everywhere with her. "Patients there who had not spoken to a human being in years spoke to Diamond," Evarts said. "They'd save bits of food for him. The head doctor kept telling me I shouldn't bring him." The doctor held a board meeting about the dog without telling Evarts. "However, the superintendent and the assistant superintendent were all friends of mine, and they all happened to have dogs," she said, then paused with a slow grin. "Diamond won."[9]

She simply had no truck with bureaucracies when they put budgets and rules before humanity. In the 1970s she fought back when the Harlem Valley State Hospital sought to save money, downsize and move its patients elsewhere. "They didn't know what they were doing," she said, "and I just told them to stay out. They were sending people through the buildings to pick out patients to transfer. I called them up on the hospital telephone and said, 'You better not come to Building B,' and they didn't."[10] But not long afterwards, the state began to move patients, declaring that the buildings they were in were not safe, though some had had major renovations. Four hundred patients, those without families, were moved. Jo said her reaction was "rage." She said she imagined "some of them will die, the lucky ones, that is. They won't be lonely. The majority were completely upset and depressed, wondering what was going to happen to them. Some of them were very devoted to the building. Some of them had lived in B for over 30 years."[11]

By the 1970s, when she was in her 60s, she was one of the few doctors to practice in the Harlem Valley and likely the only one who charged $10 for an office visit if you felt like paying it. She rarely sent out bills. And instead of cash, she accepted food off of the farm. Plus she still made house calls. She said there were four words that were the most important in medicine: "I'll be right over."

Evarts would be a doctor so long that she would go on to deliver the grandchildren of children she had delivered—many of them born at home, a practice she supported when other doctors insisted on hospital births. "I don't see why mothers should not have children where they want to," she said. She had no children of her own but considered all of the ones she delivered as her children. And she would be their advocate. If a baby born out of wedlock was not wanted, she would arrange to find a couple who wanted the baby without going through the usual social agency channels. "I used to be known as the Grey Market to Social Services of Connecticut. They disliked me intensely, but they didn't call me the Black Market because I didn't profit from it."

And while she did not hesitate to break rules when she thought it appropriate, she also venerated institutions like marriage because she so often saw its impact on children when it failed. "Love frequently gets cured by marriage," she used to say. But she would rail, striking her fist on the arm of her chair, about married couples who "have no patience, no concern about anyone but themselves. I have nasty things to say to the person whose idea it is to split. 'Tell me, if your child was playing in the driveway while you came home with the car, would you run over his legs and break them?' It didn't occur to them they didn't mind breaking his heart and robbing him of a parent."[12]

Sharing Her Life

She came late to that institution herself. She first married Dr. Gilbert Tabor in 1947, a fellow doctor on the staff at Sharon Hospital in Sharon, Conn. They lived and practiced in Millerton. And people still remember them walking hand in hand around the village—a soft counterpoint to her occasional ferocity. After he died ten years later, she established the Tabor Foundation, which has sent dozens of needy children to college for medical training and is now entrusted to the Berkshire Taconic Community Foundation to offer scholarships for education or training in a health care field to individuals who intend to work in that field afterwards in northwestern Litchfield County in Connecticut or northeastern Dutchess County. There were times in her career when Jo was the only doctor readily available in those areas. She wanted to give an incentive to others to serve it as well.

In 1960 she married Charles "Chuck" Demarest, a pianist who headed the music department at The Hotchkiss School in Lakeville, Connecticut. Chuck would have to get used to Jo's unexpected visitors, since patients showed up at all hours at their house. But, like her, he would be up early practicing on one of his grand pianos by 7 a.m. Their stove always had a soup in the making—a pot on perpetual simmer where leftovers, bones and scraps would be thrown in—nothing was wasted. When the entrance hallway needed wallpaper, Jo covered it with maps that had come as inserts into the National Geographic magazine. Many party conversations began in that hallway because someone had been or wished they had been somewhere spotted on a map. The couple had a perfect formula for welcoming their frequent guests: a warm fire in the iron stove in the den, good cocktails, lots of storytelling with the occasional bawdy joke, a meal usually built around a fine roast and vegetables from the garden, guaranteed laughter.

In her dress, Jo preferred comfort over fashion. In winter she wore snuggies, long underwear that came to the knees. Once, in the middle of visiting hours at the hospital, she was advocating for them to a shy nurse supervisor and whipped up her skirt to show them to her. Her idea of clothes shopping was to go to the local thrift shop. She favored cotton and flannel shirts, corduroys and over-the-knee skirts. Items did not have to match. She once attended a Vassar alumnae tea where the former college President Sarah Blanding described her appearance as "something the cat dragged in."[13]

Both of Jo's husbands tried to improve her taste by getting her outfits from tasteful New York City shops so she had something to wear for a night on the town. And she would on occasion do that and sometimes surprise her patients accordingly. Thuvia Hawver, who had lived in Millerton, remembered when her sister was in labor at Sharon Hospital and Dr. Jo arrived, dressed up from a dinner party and wearing a green hat with pheasant feathers on it. She delivered the baby. As for the hat, Hawver said, "She kept it on the whole time."

Public Life

In May 1980, when the Dutchess County Legislature named her senior citizen of the year and asked her to come to Poughkeepsie to accept the award, her initial reaction at age 78 was "if they were really interested in the aged, they would not make me travel to Poughkeepsie," a 35-mile drive from her Millerton, N.Y., office and four more miles from her Lakeville, Conn. home. She felt the Harlem Valley, where many county services had been scarce, had always been treated as a stepchild by Poughkeepsie, the county seat, and she suggested secession to Connecticut. Ella T. Grasso, governor of Connecticut at the time, said she was happy to discuss the idea. Dr. Jo eventually showed up at the legislative office building for her honor and got three standing ovations.

Despite the demands of her practice, Jo gave back to her community in other ways. She won a seat as a Millerton village trustee in 1960, running as a Democrat, which made front-page news in the *Poughkeepsie New Yorker* since Republicans had always dominated. More than that, she became the first woman to be elected to the village board. In 1955, she was chair of the Citizens Advisory Committee to the Webutuck School District and was an advocate for building a new junior-senior high school. In 1970 when she heard that a day care center being run in a church basement in Millerton needed permanent housing, she bought them a house.

Conclusion

Hannah Jamin, who used to live in Sharon, Conn., wrote in a letter to the editor to the *Poughkeepsie Journal* in 1979, in response to articles about Dr. Evarts:

> She stands out as a beacon for the entire medical profession to emulate. She is a G.P. who practices medicine with humanity. Her devotion to her career and her patients is known to all who have been treated by her, or have been touched by her down-to-earth philosophy of life, love and living.[14]

Jo kept practicing despite being a patient herself. In 1968 she found she had breast cancer, and was not surprised since most of her family had had cancer. But she lived with it, only taking treatment that would not get in the way of her practice. More than a decade after the diagnosis, she said, laughing a bit, "No one knows what to project about me. I've lived entirely too long with it," but then she added, "I think the human spirit is extremely important. People who don't want to live fold their tents quite quickly."[15]

Dr. Carnes Weeks, a longtime colleague at Sharon, would tell the story of how Jo, driving to her office in Dover, fell asleep at the wheel and ran into a tree, breaking her hip. After the ambulance got her to the hospital, everyone in the emergency room was on edge. They knew she was badly injured and already at risk from cancer. One doctor, nervous and desperate to lighten the mood, said, "This is the first time I've taken the pants off a lady." To which, Jo, in pain and near shock, boomed out, "Well, I'm certainly not a lady."[16]

Late in life, she answered a Vassar Alumnae form question on whether she was still professionally employed by saying: "Still practicing medicine on any patient who will stand still long enough." And she did just that until a few weeks before she died on April 7, 1983 at age 81.

Death for her was not to be feared. "Death as a rule comes as a friend, not as an enemy," she said. "I don't like it when teenage kids go out and murder themselves on the highway—it's terrible—but when you're 85 years old, and your quality of life is minus one, then death is fine. You get accustomed to the idea that death is essential—just as important as life. Think how crowded the world would be if there weren't any death. I never blame things on God. I'm sure God has his finger in the pie."[17]

Epilogue from the author: My first job out of college was editor of *The News*, a weekly newspaper based in Millerton that covered the Harlem Valley. New to town, I had not been able to find an affordable apartment and the temporary housing I had was suddenly coming to an end. People in town suggested that I speak to Dr. Evarts, whom I had heard of but not yet met. I went to her office, introduced myself and asked if she knew anyone renting a room. She looked up at me over her glasses and said, "Come live with us." I had just met her. She didn't know me at all. I sputtered something along the lines of "Well, I couldn't impose like that." She then glared at me and said, "What's wrong with us?" I think that my mouth was just open at that point. She told me where she lived in Lakeville and to come when I was ready. The door was not locked. Just come in. And so I did.

---

[1] Parts of this article were originally researched and written by this author and published in the *Poughkeepsie Journal*. Meg Alexander (now Meg Downey), A talk with 'Dr. Jo,' *Poughkeepsie Journal*, Sept. 16, 1979, pp. 1B, 5B

[2] Teddie Burnett, At 78, Dr. Jo still makes house calls, Poughkeepsie Journal, Sept. 16, 1979, p. 1B

[3] Eunice Trowbridge and April Radbill, "Dr. Josephine Evarts, A Tribute," 1981, p. 3

[4] Eunice Trowbridge, p. 26

[5] Meg Alexander, p. 5B

[6] Meg Alexander, p. 5B

[7] Eunice Trowbridge, pp. 42-43

[8] Eunice Trowbridge, p. 74

[9] Meg Alexander, p. 5B

[10] Meg Alexander, p. 5B

[11] Christopher Klose, Some Crying, Some Smiling As Patient Transfer Begins, *Poughkeepsie Journal*, May 11, 1971, p. 1A

[12] Meg Alexander, pp. 1B, 5B

[13] Eunice Trowbridge, p. 49

[14] Hannah Jamin, letter to the editor, Articles on Dr. Evarts lauded, *Poughkeepsie Journal*, Sept. 24, 1979, p. 4

[15] Meg Alexander, p. 5B

[16] Teddie Burnett, pp. 1B, 16B

[17] Meg Alexander, p. 5B

Franny Reese
"Defender of the Hudson Valley"

by Molly B. Jones

"Frances Reese, 85, Defender of Hudson Valley": so proclaimed the headline on her obituary in *The New York Times* on July 9, 2003. "Valley 'Visionary' Dies," read the *Poughkeepsie Journal*'s headline. "Service set for 'Soul of the Hudson Valley,'" said the *Times Herald-Record* in Middletown, New York. "River loses one of its treasures," the *Albany Times Union* wrote.[1]

In fact, Franny Reese's lasting contribution to history reverberates far beyond the region where she lived. Her unwavering commitment as a leader in the 17-year battle to defeat the construction of a huge hydropower plant on Storm King Mountain resulted in a landmark decision that is considered to be the basis of modern environmental law in the *United States: Scenic Hudson Preservation Conference v. Federal Power Commission.*

Figure 1. Franny Reese, "Defender of the Hudson Valley," here seated at the edge of her beloved Hudson River with Storm King Mountain in the background. N.d. Photograph. Collection of Scenic Hudson, New York.

Franny Reese and the Storm King Fight

The distinctive face of the Hudson Highland's most prominent mountain rises from the river on the west bank. Across from Breakneck Ridge on the east, creating a dramatic gorge, the mountain would have been forever scarred if the developer, Consolidated Edison, had been able to build the project. The first river valley residents intent on preserving the beauty of the Highlands met in 1963 to see what they could do to stop the project. Soon after, six founders organized what became Scenic Hudson. The new nonprofit organization went to court to challenge the Power Commission's approval of plans to build the plant.

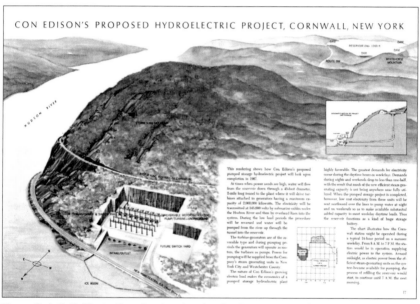

Figure 2. Artist's illustration showing the plan for the new plant, from the Consolidated Edison 1962 Annual Report. Collection of Scenic Hudson, New York.

In 1965, Scenic Hudson had a big win: the U.S. Second Circuit Court of Appeals in New York ruled to annul the permit for Con Ed to proceed until studies of the plant's impact on the area's scenery were completed. The effects of the plant's operation on fish in the river were also to be studied. The precedent set by the ruling was groundbreaking: no longer did citizens need to have a monetary investment in a piece of land to sue as a plaintiff for its conservation. "Renewed proceedings must include as a basic concern the preservation of natural beauty and national historic sites, keeping in mind that in our affluent society, the cost of a project is only one of several factors to be considered," the decision said. The renewed hearings took four years and, in 1971, the Court of Appeals reversed the 1965 ruling and upheld Con Ed's permit.

This was only the beginning of the first of many twists and turns through the courts. "There were definitely times when we were discouraged," says Albert Butzel, the well-known environmental lawyer who began working just after the Federal Power Commission licensed the plant and stayed on through a dozen decisions from the first to the final "peace treaty" in 1980.

> In 1971, we lost before the Court of Appeals, and people lost interest in the case. It became difficult to raise money. Franny Reese stayed as the strength of the organization [Scenic Hudson]. She generally held the organization together when the prospects for winning were very bleak, and later she took on a new role as the organization became the leader of the environmental movement in the Hudson Valley. Franny was amazing. What she accomplished was remarkable, and she deservedly got credit for it.[2]

Figure 3. Franny Reese, chair of Scenic Hudson, and Robert H. Boyle, chair of the Hudson River Fishermen's Association (now Riverkeeper), both wearing glasses, sign the "Peace Treaty on the Hudson" with Con Edison's Charles Luce, New York Attorney General Robert Abrams, and (standing) Russel Train, Environmental Protection Agency Administrator. 1980. Photograph. Collection of Scenic Hudson.

The ruling stated that groups with "special interest in aesthetic, conservational, and recreational aspects" had legal standing as an "aggrieved" party. Language from the ruling was incorporated into the National Environmental Policy Act, which established the Environmental Protection Agency and mandated environmental impact studies for certain construction projects. From the growing awareness of environmental issues raised by the Storm King case came a long list of other laws, including the Clean Water Act.

Scenic Hudson after Storm King

After Scenic Hudson finally won the case, the organization might have declared victory and disbanded. Instead, its board of directors decided to broaden its mission by engaging in other environmental issues affecting the river. Franny, who had chaired the board since 1966, continued in the leadership role until 1984. During her tenure, the Scenic Hudson Land Trust was established with a substantial gift from DeWitt and Lila Acheson Wallace, co-founders and publishers of the *Reader'sDigest*. Four marshes along the river with a combined total of 3,500 acres were conserved as National Estuarine Research Reserves.

> Today, Scenic Hudson is nationally renowned for its success in creating riverfront parks and preserves from New York City to the Adirondacks. In recent years, the organization has continued to oppose developmental threats to the valley, but it also became a champion of efforts that would improve the quality of life for residents. It has been aggressive in promoting land conservation, farmland preservation, land-use planning, and the protection and improvement of environmental quality, including pollution controls and cleaning up PCBs in the riverbed.[3]

Franny Reese State Park

In the year of Franny Reese's death, Scenic Hudson purchased 253 acres on the west side of the river south of the Mid-Hudson Bridge connecting Poughkeepsie and Highland to keep the land from residential development. Four years later, the State of New York's Office of Parks, Recreation, and Historic Preservation purchased the property and named it Franny Reese State Park. The park, which is managed by Scenic Hudson, has nearly three miles of trails which intersect with the Loop Trail connecting the Walkway Over the Hudson and the Mid-Hudson Bridge, offering exhilarating views of the river she loved.

"Franny Reese State Park is a very good example of the kind of collaboration that Scenic Hudson has been able to accomplish," says her son Alexander. "Very important land along the river has been saved for the public."[4]

Franny: Famous for Her Energy

Frances Gallatin Stevens, known to everyone as "Franny," was born in Manhattan in 1917 and raised in rural Somerset County, New Jersey. In 2003, she was fatally injured in an automobile accident on Route 9 not far from Obercreek, her home in Hughsonville, an unincorporated hamlet in the Town of Wappinger. Her advancing years had not slowed her commitment to Scenic Hudson and the many other organizations she supported. Her energy, for which she was famous, did not appear diminished, either. "She was in the prime of her life at 85," said Scenic Hudson President Ned Sullivan at the time of her death. "She was going strong."[5]

Although best known for her commitment to Scenic Hudson, Franny dedicated her energy to a number of other causes. A year or two before her death, she told a friend that she was, at that time, serving on 44 boards.[6] "She was a very incisive thinker and strategic planner," says Mary Flad, who worked with her to find a future for the Maple Grove estate in Poughkeepsie. "She was important on so many boards. She could come in with the vision and her checkbook and make things happen. Her untimely death was a blow to the Maple Grove project."[7]

"Franny was a wizard at how she could draw you in to volunteer on one of her projects," says Mary Lunt, who became friends with Franny when they played doubles at the Poughkeepsie Tennis Club. "Once she got to know you, she would figure out what would interest you. You had to be absolutely determined to say 'No' to her."[8] Mary and her husband, Bill, came up with a project of their own: saving a large orchard in the Town of Poughkeepsie from development, which became, with the support of Scenic Hudson, Peach Hill Park.

Mary Lunt is one of many women who were inspired by Franny Reese to champion projects and programs in the area. Another is Frances F. Dunwell, who has had a long and successful career in environmental conservation. She has been the coordinator of the Hudson River Estuary Program, part of the State of New York's Department of Environmental Conservation, since its beginning 30 years ago. In her book, *The Hudson: America's River*, she dedicated her work "To my family and friends, and in particular to Franny Reese, without whom, in so many ways, this book could not have been written."[9] Still another inspired by Franny was the late Klara Sauer, who for 20 years (1979-1999) was executive director of Scenic Hudson. During her tenure, the organization grew from a three-person office with a $65,000 budget to a staff 10 times as large and a $2 million budget.[10]

> Under the aegis of its effective and indomitable leadership, Franny Reese and Klara Sauer, Scenic Hudson adopted an ambitious mission that led to a proactive engagement in preserving the distinctive landscape, history, and culture of the Hudson Valley. Through initiatives that have preserved farmland and places of distinctive scenic or historical significance, as well as its efforts to develop riverside parks in cities and secure greater public access to the river, Scenic Hudson has become the most important conservation organization in the Hudson River Valley and surely one of the most consequential in the United States.[11]

Franny's Other Causes and Projects

Francesca Olivieri, one of Franny's granddaughters, recalls that her grandmother loved to play tennis. "She could place the ball so perfectly," she remembers. "She was really consistent. I have a theory that tennis is a window into your personality. She was unassuming but so effective."[12] The lawyer Albert Butzel agrees that she was unassuming, but says that's not why she was successful in her work. "She was as tough as nails," he says. "She knew what she thought should be done, and she saw that it was done."[13]

Among the local organizations Franny served: Marist College, Locust Grove, the Boscobel Restoration, the Grinnell Library in Wappingers Falls, and the Stewart Airport Commission. She was an active member and supporter of Zion Episcopal Church in Wappingers Falls. Farther afield, in Manhattan, where she kept an apartment, she volunteered for Columbia Presbyterian Hospital and is credited with helping save the historic early twentieth century mansion now called The House of the Redeemer, a New York City landmark.

Her awards include the Eleanor Roosevelt Val-Kill Medal; the Governor's Parks and Preservation Award; the Historic Hudson Valley Award for Land Conservation; the New York State Bar Association Award for Advocacy of Environmental Causes; the Marist College President's Award; and the Mid-Hudson Pattern for Progress Award.

"A teacher at heart, Franny taught us to see the Hudson Valley's exceptional beauty and reminded us that we are its stewards,"Dennis J. Murray, the president of Marist College, said. "Her life was a special gift to us all."[14] President Murray was quoted as telling the author in an article shortly after she died: Franny Reese, as vice president of the Marist board and chairwoman of student affairs, bridged the generation gap effortlessly. Her interest in art and architecture extended to the design of the college's library, a prominent building on the river. "I think Franny had a unique appreciation for beauty, whether it be the beauty of the river, the beauty in the Hudson Highlands, in a building, or in a tree," Murray said.[15]

Franny came to be involved in Locust Grove, a large property on a bluff south of Poughkeepsie overlooking the river, as a result of her marriage to Willis Reese. The land was owned in the 1700s by Henry Livingston, Jr., a member of the prominent pre-Revolutionary War family, from whom Willis was descended. After ownership of the property passed to a not-for-profit educational foundation in 1975, Willis served on the board of directors, and after his death, Franny joined the board. During her tenure as chair, she promoted the idea to feature information on Samuel F. B. Morse, who had built a mansion on the bluff in 1850. The visitors' center built during her tenure contains a gallery dedicated to Morse's life and work as an artist and inventor.[16]

Franny's Early Life

Remembering what she knew of her mother's childhood, her only daughter, Frances Reese Olivieri, says that her mother believed that her parents were disappointed when, nine years after her sister and only sibling was born, she was not a boy. She was named for her father, Francis. "She had some learning disabilities," Frances Olivieri says. "Her mother worked with her. She was left handed, and she was made to write with her right hand. She had a wonderful sense of direction but her understanding— the way she explained directions—was totally backwards."[17]

Somerset County, where she was raised, was then (and is now) famous for its horse farms. "Mum was an excellent rider, and she was sent to Foxcroft School in Virginia for boarding school, which was known for its riding. She was unhappy there, though, until she was allowed to have a dog."

Frances Olivieri remembers her mother telling stories about spending summers as a child with her family in Murray Bay (now La Malbaie), Quebec, making beds of evergreen branches. "She loved the out-of-doors," she says. "She appreciated the beauty of the natural world, and she knew a great deal of natural history. She knew the names of all the mosses, for example."

Her Love for the Arts

Franny Reese's early interest in nature was matched by her appreciation for and desire to create art. After studying playwriting and English at Barnard College, she attended Yale Art School. During her lifetime, she wrote plays and poetry. Her watercolor paintings were known to her friends and family and were often featured on her Christmas cards. She learned metalworking and pottery. "Mum was always doing some kind of artwork," Frances Olivieri says. "We were taking a drawing class together when she died."

Figure 4. Painting of a raccoon and mallards by Franny Reese originally installed in her son Bill's bathroom at Obercreek. Oil on canvas. Photograph by Molly B. Jones. Collection of Frances Reese Olivieri.

Convinced of the importance of nineteenth century Hudson River School landscape paintings to American cultural history, Franny persuaded the Metropolitan Museum of Art to commission and publish *The Hudson River and Its Paintings* (American Legacy Press, 1972), a large, handsome illustrated book that renewed interest in and appreciation for this period of art history. The author, John K. Howat, curator at the Met and later head of the museum's American Wing, dedicated the book to Storm King Mountain and the Hudson River Gorge and contributed all royalties to Scenic Hudson. The book was useful in the legal argument to save Storm King Mountain from disfigurement.[18]

While she enjoyed traditional art forms, she had fun with her creativity. "She was incredibly inventive," her daughter remembers. She painted a series of animals and birds on panels mounted in her son Bill's bathroom. "The bathtub had a beaver, and there were rabbits and birds." When the panels were taken down, Frances Olivieri kept a few. "She was wonderful with Halloween costumes, too," she says. "One year she made me a pussy willow costume, and I won the prize as 'most beautiful.' Another year two of my brothers were two poles with a clothesline strung between them and squares of fabric hanging like laundry that spelled out "I LOVE YOU.'"

Franny and Willis

Franny was married at age 19 to Willis Livingston Mesier Reese, who went on to a distinguished career as a law professor at Columbia University and the director of the Parker School of Foreign and Comparative Law for 25 years. Her husband shared her interest in conservation and historic preservation. "They were a marvelous pair," says Mary Richardson Miller. "Brilliant, both of them, and devoted to each other."[19] In addition to their daughter, Frances, they had four sons: William, John, George, and Alexander.

Mary Miller knew Franny and Willis when they were neighbors for a time in Hewlett, Long Island. With their five children, the Reese family lived in Hewlett during the week, as Willis' commute was more convenient than traveling from Dutchess County. "Every Friday we would drive up here to Wappingers," remembers Alexander Reese, the youngest of the children, "and every Sunday we would drive back." He remembers when his father managed a milking herd on the Obercreek property, after which a local farmer raised Hereford cattle and corn.[20]

Obercreek

Willis Reese died in 1990.[21] Franny died in 2003. After the death of his mother, Alex, who was living nearby on Wheeler Hill Road, bought out his siblings' share of the main house and adjoining 30 acres. Today, he and his wife operate a certified organic farm and brewery, and he serves on the board of the Glynwood Center for Regional Food and Farming. Based in Cold Spring, the nonprofit organization advocates for local food production in the Hudson Valley and beyond. "I think Mum would be very happy with what Alex has done at Obercreek," says his sister Frances Olivieri.

The original structure on what became the Obercreek estate was built in 1856 by William H. Willis and has now been in the family for six generations, undergoing a series of additions and renovations. The house is a blend of architectural styles most recently modified by Alex's wife, Alison Spear, an architect.[22] Unchanged is a magnificent Gothic Revival chapel on the second floor carved from red oak by the Russian-American sculptor Gleb W. Derujinsky, which was commissioned by Willis Reese's mother. (A side note: His father, William Willis Reese, was president of the Dutchess County Historical Society from 1928 until his death in 1942.)

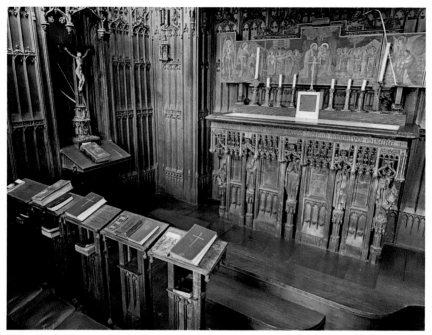

Figure 5. The Reese family chapel at Obercreek. Photograph by Alexander Reese.

The Episcopal Bishop of New York, The Right Rev. Andrew ML Dietsche, tells of being shown the chapel after Franny Reese's funeral, when a reception was held on the lawn at Obercreek. "Her prayer book and her glasses were there, just as she had left them," he recalls. "She had her questions, but she was devoted to the practices of the Christian tradition."[23] Her family recalls that she was in the chapel nearly every day. Before her death, she specified that if the home were ever sold to someone outside the family, the chapel would be removed and reinstalled in an appropriate location for prayer and meditation.

Judith Barba, who worshiped with Franny at Zion Church, remembers the funeral well. As anticipated, the congregation could not all be seated in the church's pews, and the overflow crowd filled the Parish Hall, where the service was piped in. "The music director asked me if I would sing in the choir for the service," Judith recalls. "She said, 'That way you're sure to get a seat.'"[24] The night before the funeral, when visiting hours were held, there was "a line of hundreds of people stretching out to the street waiting to greet the family and pay their respects," remembers Mary Flad.[25]

Franny's Legacy

Like his mother, Alex Reese is active in historic preservation and environmental affairs. Before her death, they had overlapping terms on the board of Boscobel House and Gardens near Garrison. "My mother was interested not only in the historic house but also in the wildlife trail to Constitution Marsh," Alex says. "It was a pleasure to work with her." [26] In recent years, Alex has taken a leadership position at Scenic Hudson, the organization most closely associated with his mother's name, currently serving as a member of the Board of Directors and vice-chairman of the Scenic Hudson Land Trust. "I've had all sorts of different positions at Scenic Hudson," he says. "I've been very much involved in the Scenic Hudson mission. It's in my DNA."

Last summer, two members of the family's next generation—teenage sons of Alex's nieces—worked on the Obercreek Farm. "They weeded and watered and worked to remove invasive plants," says Augusta Reese Donohue, one of Franny's granddaughters.

Augusta lives in Cold Spring Harbor on Long Island and is a member of the executive board of the North Shore Land Alliance. Her cousin, Francesca Olivieri, has served on the board of Scenic Hudson. The cousins received their activist training by spending time with their grandmother at Obercreek when they were children. "We were always going off to something," Augusta recalls, "a fundraiser, or a park opening, or a clean-up. We went to Boscobel, we went to Storm King. I didn't know why we were doing these things—I didn't have the big picture at that time. Now I know that these were very valuable experiences for me."[27]

Also, she remembers, no matter what the weather, her grandmother insisted on taking a walk every day. "I'd say, 'Granny, it's raining,' and she'd say, 'There are boots in the closet.' I remember once I was at Obercreek—I was about 18—and Granny said 'We need to go tobogganing.' I didn't want to go to the effort of blazing the toboggan path, so she did it, and we went sledding. She was well into her 70s at the time. " Her death was "shocking and horrible," Augusta says. "She wasn't slowing down in any way."

Scenic Hudson's Ned Sullivan, who at the time of her death said that Franny was "in her prime" when she died at age 85, says today:

While I miss the sage advice and caring spirit of Franny Reese, I and many of my Scenic Hudson colleagues continue to be guided by her passion for preserving the Hudson Valley's natural and historic treasures. She possessed boundless energy and an infectious, can-do attitude that kept Scenic Hudson afloat during our long campaign to prevent construction of the Storm King hydroelectric plant. After that victory, she encouraged the organization to reach new heights—creating riverfront parks, protecting views from Olana, halting new threats to the river, and commencing our farmland protection program. We all benefit from Franny's powerful legacy—a valley whose natural beauty remains available for all to explore.[28]

---

[1] Wolfgang Saxon, "Frances Reese, 85, Defender of the Hudson Valley," *The New York Times*, July 30, 2003; See also Dan Shapley, "Frances Reese, 1918-2003: Valley Visionary Dies," *Poughkeepsie Journal*, July 4, 2003; Wayne A. Hall, "Service set for 'soul of the Hudson Valley,'" *Times Herald-Record*, Middletown, NY, copy of newspaper clipping, date not known; David S. Sampson, "River loses one of its treasures," *Albany Times-Union*, July 24, 2003.

[2] Albert K. Butzel, interview by author, telephone and email, January 21, February 22, and March 1, 2020.

[3] David Schuyler, *Embattled River: The Hudson and Modern American Environmentalism,* (New York: Cornell University Press, 2018), p. 141.

[4] Alexander Reese, interview by author, telephone, February 21 and 25, 2020.

[5] Wayne A. Hall, Ibid.

[6] Candace Lewis, interview by author, Poughkeepsie, August 12, 2019.

[7] Mary Flad, interview by author, email, February 19, 2020.

[8] Mary W. Lunt, interview by author, telephone, January 30, 2020.

[9] Frances F. Dunwell, *The Hudson: America's River*, (New York: Columbia University Press, 2008, expanded and updated edition of *The Hudson River Highlands*, 1991).

[10] John Ferro, "Klara Sauer, leading Voice of environmental movement, dies," *Poughkeepsie Journal*, 24 June, 2015.

[11] David Schuyler, Ibid., pp. 131-132.

[12] Francesca Olivieri, interview by author, telephone, January 31, 2020.

[13] Albert K. Butzel, Ibid.

[14] Scenic Hudson, *Franny Reese State Park: Park Guide and Trail Map*, undated.

[15] Dan Shapley, Ibid.

[16] Kenneth Snodgrass, interview by author, telephone, February 7, 2020

[17] Frances Reese Olivieri, interview by author, Frances Olivieri's home, January 25, 2020.

[18] David Schuyler, Ibid., pp. 21-22.

[19] Mary Richardson Miller, interview by author, telephone, January 16, 2020

[20] Alexander Reese, Ibid..

[21] Peter B. Flint, "Willis Reese, 77, Professor and Expert in International Law," *The New York Times*, 11 July 11, 1990.

[22] Nina Griscom, "Alison Spear Renovates a Historic Farmhouse in Upstate New York," *Architectural Digest*, March 15, 2017 (reprinted from June 2013 issue).

[23] The Rt. Rev. Andrew ML Dietsche, interview by author, author's home, November 24, 2019.

[24] Judith I. Barba, interview by author, telephone, January 8, 2020.

[25] Mary Flad, Ibid.

[26] Alexander Reese, Ibid.

[27] Augusta Reese Donohue, interview by author, telephone, February 7, 2020.

[28] Ned Sullivan, statement provided to author, email, February 7, 2020.

ARTICLES

Reflection in the Glass Doorway: The Mystery Man Behind the Van Tine Postcards

by Diane Lapis

I have always admired the beautiful printed postcards of Beacon, New York: Mt. Beacon with its majestic views of the Hudson River, the Fishkill Creek, and Main Street's stately brick buildings. This Fishkill Creek Falls postcard scene is simple and direct, showing natural wonders and man-made structures found in the area (Figure 1).

FISHKILL CREEK FALLS, BEACON, N. Y.   53931

Figure 1. Postcard of Fishkill Creek Falls, Beacon, N.Y., early twentieth century.

Picturesque views like these were made as souvenirs for travelers to the Hudson Valley. But it was the photographer's artistic vision that captured time in a frame for today's inhabitants to hold dear.

But who, I've wondered, was the image maker for these century-old post-cards? While some real photo postcards include the photographer's name as part of the caption, printed cards rarely identify their creator. As an inveterate collector of postcards and a local historian, I set out to discover the photographer behind these artistic images.

In some instances, the postcard photographer was born and raised in the area, with a penchant for photography. In other cases, it was an itinerant photographer traveling through town with camera in tow. Clues about the producer are often provided on the flip side of the postcard. The inscription on the left edge may list those involved in its production such as the publisher, distributor, printer, sales rep, or photographer, as well as a logo and copyright. By studying a collection of cards from a specific geographic area, we may be able to tease out the story of the postcard photographer while learning more about the life of the town and its cultural and architectural heritage.

Van Tine Printed Postcards (1902-1941)

One group of printed cards of Beacon, and its antecedent villages of Fishkill Landing and Matteawan, includes four different inscriptions, united by a common element: R.T. Van Tine Fishkill Landing, R.T. Van Tine Fishkill-on-Hudson, R.T. Van Tine, Beacon NY, and Van Tines, Beacon (Figure 2). An analysis of cards from the Beacon Historical Society and the Historical Society of Newburgh Bay and the Highlands and other private collections has revealed 220 Van Tine produced cards printed between 1902 and 1941.

Over 70 of the images are of Mt. Beacon—the Incline Railway, the Beaconcrest Hotel and Casino, the cottages, and the DAR Monument. Other subjects include the Fishkill Creek, the Hudson River, local schools, churches, firehouses, hotels, factories, the railroad station, Main Street, the Post Office, Memorial Hall, the Veteran's Hospital at Castle Point, Mat-

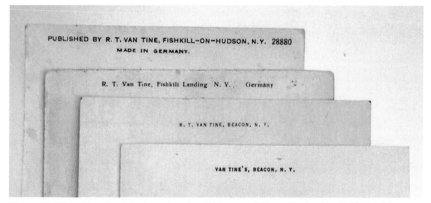

Figure 2. Flip side of printed postcards of Beacon, NY, published by R. T. Van Tine. Collection of Diane and Peter Lapis.

teawan State Hospital for the Criminally Insane and views of Newburgh. It is not surprising that Van Tine cards catered to both locals (pictures of local schools and other important buildings) and tourists (scenes of Mt. Beacon and hotels on Main Street), as postcards provided an inexpensive way of communicating both within a town and across the country.

The "Van Tines, Beacon NY" series included mostly reprints of earlier cards with the exception of newly built structures such as the Post Office, South Avenue School, and a "modern" Main Street, the latter three published in 1941. These postcards depict scenes from a tight-knit geographic area in Beacon and its neighboring communities. To date, little evidence of cards produced outside these boundaries can be found. Creating a database of the Van Tine product line has proved to be a useful tool in understanding the depth and breadth of Beacon's history and neighboring areas at the turn of the twentieth century, as well as an aid in learning about the photographer who produced the images.

Robert Van Tine—Dean of Beacon Merchants (1860-1941)

Let us return to the printed name on the flipside of the Van Tine cards... who was R.T. Van Tine and was s/he the mastermind of these iconic images of our area? We know from historical records and newspaper accounts that R.T. or Robert T. Van Tine was the proprietor of a stationery store centrally located on Main Street in Fishkill Landing, near the railroad and ferry depots, and a short walking distance from Matteawan's bustling factories. Van Tines was originally a haberdashery when it first opened in 1880. A few years later, Robert Van Tine expanded the business and moved to larger quarters, dropping the men's clothing line and instead featuring newspapers, magazines, postcards, greeting cards, sporting goods, school and office supplies, and the latest in Kodak cameras. Soon thereafter, Van Tines became the go-to place for current local and national news.

Van Tines continued to be a thriving establishment, especially after the opening of the Mt. Beacon Incline and Casino in 1902, followed by the Beaconcrest Hotel a few years later. Three factors, Robert's business acumen, the propitious timing of the Incline, and the change in the United States Postal Service regulations, led to the production of the Beacon postcards that we know today.

Beginning in 1902, the U.S. Postal Service started to allow private publishers to enter the postcard market, and provide rural free delivery, all for the cost of a penny stamp. The sale of postcards became a national craze as tourists and locals sent friends and family missives, and postcard exchange clubs formed across the country. Robert Van Tine capitalized on this opportunity by publishing postcards of local scenes, and selling these and other postcard views for "2 for 5 cents." (Figure 3)

By 1905, his wholesale and retail business was selling over one hundred thousand postcards.

Figure 3: Interior of Van Tines Stationery Store, c. 1908. Photograph. Collection of Louise Pittack.

Robert Van Tine became known as the "Dean of Beacon Merchants," maintaining a robust wholesale and retail newspaper and stationery business in Beacon for sixty-one years until his death in 1941. On many anniversaries of the founding of his store, the local papers would feature an article about the success of the business and Van Tine's dedication to local organizations. Yet, there is no mention about his photographic abilities. If Robert was the publisher and distributor of these local postcards, who was the photographer?

Harry Van Tine—News Photographer (1885- 1968)

Robert and his wife Elizabeth Moore Van Tine had one son named Harry, born in 1885. As a young man, Harry clerked at the Van Tines store, and was proficient and productive with his camera, photographing hundreds of local scenes of Beacon, Cold Spring and Newburgh, and nearby village

Figure 4. Harry Van Tine, Exterior of Van Tines Stationery Store, December 1907. Photograph. Collection of the Beacon Historical Society. Harry Van Tine can be seen in reflection in the glass of the front door.

Figure 5. Harry Van Tine, Exterior of Van Tines Stationery Store (detail), December 1907. Photograph. Collection of the Beacon Historical Society. Harry Van Tine with his photographic equipment can be seen in reflection in the glass of the front door.

of Fishkill. The local newspaper often reported on Harry's photographic endeavors "producing many pictures suitable for postcards" Harry's reflection, camera and tripod is visible in the glass doorway at Van Tines in this photograph from 1907 (Figures 4 and 5). Glass plate negatives, discovered in the basement of Van Tines after the business closed in 1968, revealed original images of Mt. Beacon later published into postcards (Figures 6-9).

Figure 6. Harry Van Tine, Donkeys atop Mt. Beacon. Donkeys provided entertainment for guests, transported supplies, and were featured in the silent films directed by D.W. Griffith. Collection of Gene Trifolo, Sr.

Figure 7. Hand-colored postcard published by R.T. Van Tine of donkey photo taken a few seconds apart. Collection of Diane and Peter Lapis.

Figure 8. Harry Van Tine, Looking down the track from Mt. Beacon. Collection of the Beacon Historical Society.

Looking down the track from Mt. Beacon

Figure 9. Postcard published by R.T. Van Tine of the same photo. Collection of the Beacon Historical Society.

When the American Biograph Company filmed three silent movies on the summit of Mt. Beacon in 1909 and 1910, Harry was the "unofficial" still photographer capturing images of director D.W. Griffith, actors Mary Pickford and her sister Lottie, and dozens of others dressed in Native American and Civil War garb. These images were sold as postcards at Van Tines' stationery store. Harry also worked as a photographer and correspondent for the *Newburgh Daily News* from 1910-1915. His professional breakthrough came in 1913, when Harry Thaw, the convicted murderer of architect Stanford White, escaped Matteawan State Hospital for the Criminally Insane. Harry's photographs and James Forrestal Jr.'s ace reporting of Thaw's daring getaway gained national attention. (Forrestal would later become the Secretary of the Navy under F.D. Roosevelt and the first Secretary of Defense under Truman.)

Harry's photographic accomplishments at the newspaper gained him entrée into the Hearst-Selig News Pictorial in New York City as a "moving pictures" operator in 1915. Three years later, he was sent by the Hearst Company to Washington D.C. to open the International News Photo (INP) bureau. While there, Harry and a group of dedicated photographers from the major news agencies and photography studios banded together to form the White House News Photographer's Association (WHNPA) in 1922. Its mission was, and continues to be, to promote, protect, and advance the interests of its members who cover the White House and other events in Washington and beyond. Harry would serve on the board as president, vice president, secretary and treasurer over many decades. Harry's work as a White House news photographer and manager with INP, and later, Reni News Photo Service, spanned almost 50 years, photographing presidents from Wilson to Kennedy in the United States and abroad.

Harry stayed connected to Beacon throughout his illustrious career in Washington D.C. Upon his father Robert's death, Harry ran Van Tines as an absentee owner thanks to Gordon Wilson, a Beacon local, who acted as general manager (Figure 10). A few years ago, when Wilson's children sold his home, they left items on the sidewalk for trash pick-up. A neighbor, who was also the local librarian and aware of Wilson's connection to Van Tine, retrieved a box that contained letters sent to Gordon alongside hundreds of photographs by Harry and his colleagues at the INP. This discovery helped to convey the scope of Harry's work as a White House news photographer and manager.

Figure 10. Photograph of Gordon Wilson (left) and Harry (right) in front of Van Tines with examples of Harry's photographic work. Many of the images seen on display were made into postcards. Note below the numbers "1880" are photos of Harry Thaw, Evelyn Nesbitt, and Lewis Tompkins.

Conclusion

Investigating the Beacon postcards proved to be a rewarding endeavor. Harry documented his photographic career in scrapbooks that combined newspaper clippings, personal narratives, letters, and photographs, some of which were later published and distributed by his father as postcards. This body of material attests to the depth of Harry's work from his youth until his death in 1968. It was thrilling to discover and follow the span of Harry Van Tine's career, from the postcard-making days as a young man in his father's store at the turn of the century, to his later years as a professional photographer capturing images of world leaders.

---

[1] Bob Bogdan, and Todd Weseloh, *Real Photo Postcard Guide: The People's Photography*, (New York: Syracuse University Press, 2006), p. 195.

[2] Mark Werther, and Lorenzo Mott, , *Linen Postcards: Images of the American Dream*(Canada: Sentinel Publishing, 2002), p. 35.

[3] Bodgan and Weseloh, p. 196.

[4] Special thanks to David Turner, Doug Story, and Diane and Peter Lapis

[5] Rosamond B.Vaule, *As We Were: American Photographic Postcards, 1905-1930* (Boston: David R. Godine Publisher, 2004), p. 50.

[6] "Guide to Dating Curt Teich Postcards." *The Newbury Library.* www.newberry.org

[7] *Beacon News*, February 28, 1929.

[8] Alan Petrulis, "A Not So Concise History of the Evolution of Postcards in the United States." *Metropolitan Postcard Club*, www.metropostcard.com.

[9] "A Successful Business Man." *Fishkill Standard*, December 2, 1905.

[10] *Fishkill Standard*, 1905.

[11] *Beacon News*, May 8, 1927, and February 28, 1929.

[12] *Fishkill Herald*, May 7, 1904.

[13] *Fishkill Standard*, September 16,1905.

[14] *Fishkill Daily Herald*, November 6, 1909 and October 4, 1910.

[15] "Van Tine Enters the Movie Field," *The Newburgh Daily News*, September 23, 1915.

[16] Morg Hoyt, "Turning Back the Clock," *Beacon News*, April 1949.

[17] "Daily News Man In Peace Party," *The Newburgh Daily News*, November 27,1918.

[18] Dennis Brack, *Presidential Picture Stories: Behind the Cameras at the White House* (2013) p. 10.

[19] "About: Our Mission." *White House News Photographers Association*, www.whnpa.org.

ADDENDA

Contributors

Myra B. Young Armstead, Ph.D. is Lyford Paterson Edwards and Helen Gray Edwards Professor of Historical Studies and Vice President for Academic Inclusive Excellence at Bard College, Annandale-on-Hudson, New York. Her books include *Freedom's Gardener: James F. Brown, Horticulture and the Hudson Valley in Antebellum America*; and *Mighty Change, Tall Within: Black Identity in the Hudson Valley*

Eleanor Rubin Charwat. Ellie is a native of Poughkeepsie, where she attended the Poughkeepsie Day School and Poughkeepsie High School. After graduation from Cornell University where Ellie majored in government, she went to Washington, D.C. to work for President Kennedy's Committee on Juvenile Delinquency and later for Howard University.

After four years in Brazil, where husband Martin was in the Foreign Service, Ellie and Martin returned to Poughkeepsie and raised their two children. Ellie got involved in many community organizations: the League of Women Voters, Eleanor Roosevelt Center at Val-Kill, United Way, the Arlington Rotary Club, Literacy Volunteers, Oakwood Friends School, the Dutchess County Historical Society, and the Poughkeepsie Public Library District. Ellie worked at Marist College for 13 years as head of the School of Adult Education and taught political science as an adjunct faculty member. She was also elected to two terms on the Poughkeepsie Town Board.

Ellie is the author of T*he League of Women Voters in Dutchess County, New York: 1925–1990*, P*rohibition in the Hudson Valley: Along the Bootleg Trail, Small Town Lawyer: Highlights of Nathaniel Rubin's Career* about her father; and a memoir *A Life Well-Lived*.

Meg Downey, chief marketing officer at Omega Institute, a nonprofit educational and retreat center, in Rhinebeck, N.Y., spent most of her career as a journalist. A two-time Pulitzer Prize finalist, Downey was executive editor and editorial page editor of the *Poughkeepsie Journal* and managing editor of the Tennessean in Nashville. She began her career as editor of *The Millerton News*. Downey has won more than 40 national journalism awards. She has been an editor and contributing writer for 10 books, a magazine editor, and a television news co-host. She also taught a journalism seminar at Vassar College for nine years.

She serves on the boards of Hudson River Foundation, the Hudson River Valley Greenway Communities Council, the North East Historical Society and the Millerton Cinema Arts and Cultural Center. A graduate of Smith College, Downey lives in Millerton with her husband, Edward, an attorney and certified financial planner.

Barbara Hughey is a Land Stewardship Consultant working with private and institutional clients to enhance environmental health and biodiversity in the landscape through projects and public education. She has forty years of experience in ecological landscape design, native and medicinal plant restoration, organic agriculture, and the development of pollinator and wildlife habitat. She has completed several related courses of study including a degree in Plant and Soil Science from Cornell University, a certificate in Advanced Herbal Studies, Land Use Planning training, Biodiversity Assessment training, as well as ongoing field botany studies.

Bill Jeffway tis the Executive Director of the Dutchess County Historical Society. His first foray into local history involved his joining the Historical Society of his hometown, Northampton, Massachusetts, at age 13. He earned a BA in American Studies and English from Weslyan University before embarking on a 30-year career at the advertising agency, Ogivly & Mather. He worked in their New York, London, Singapore and Los Angeles offices developing communications for American Express, IBM and Cisco Systems.

Bill is a former Trustee of the Putnam (County) History Museum and currently a Board Member of Historic Red Hook. He was recently elected to a town council position in Milan, NY, where he had prior served as municipal historian. His book, "This Place Called Milan," marks the town's bicentennial.

He seeks to broaden community interest in local history, especially through digital communications. He founded an advisory group called, "History Speaks," which as the name implies, promotes understanding and appreciation of local history through innovative research and communications.

Molly B. Jones worked as reporter-researcher for *Time* magazine and as a general assignment reporter and, later, arts and entertainment editor for the *Anchorage Daily News*. She lives in Poughkeepsie.

Diane Lapis, ihas collected postcards for the past thirty years and revels in unveiling the hidden stories behind each image. For the past eight years, Diane has been unearthing the postcards and photographic oeuvre of Harry Van Tine. She loves to travel and visit historic places. Diane is an independent researcher and President of the Beacon Historical Society where she researches, writes, and presents topics on local history. She coauthored the book *Cocktails Across America: A Postcard View of Cocktail Culture in the 1930s, 40s, and 50s* with Anne Peck-Davis. Diane and her husband live in Beacon, NY.

Diane O'Leary practiced law in Poughkeepsie, New York for over 30 years. Admitted to practice in 1984, she had the good fortune to become a member of the new partnership of Guernsey Butts Ostertag & O'Leary in 1991 and, in 1995, the partnership of Ostertag & O'Leary. Concentrating her practice in Family and Matrimonial Law, she aspired to provide excellent representation while guiding her clients through their most painful times with civility, dignity and respect.

Early on she was active in the Dutchess County Bar Association, particularly in its Pro Bono efforts and successes, and was President of the Mid-Hudson Women's Bar Association for two terms. She was a member of the Battered Women's Panel in Family Court, lectured on issues of Family Law in the community and taught Family Law in the Paralegal Program at Marist College. In 1990, in recognition of her service to the profession and to the community, she received the New York State Bar Association's Young Lawyer of the Year award. Throughout her career she continued giving her time and sharing her expertise serving on local boards and various county and state bar task forces and committees including the New York State Bar Association's House of Delegates, the Ninth Judicial District's Judicial Screening Committee and the Marist College Paralegal Advisory Board.

She and her partner, Robert Ostertag, are now retired from their firm, now Ostertag O'Leary Barrett & Faulkner, with gratitude and pride as her daughter, Sharon Faulkner, and her protegee, Maura Barrett, recognized by their peers as premier Matrimonial Attorneys, continue the highest standards of practice.

Sandra Opdycke, Ph.D. is a retired historian. She recently published *When Women Won the Vote*, about the woman suffrage movement. She has also written books about the flu epidemic of 1918, the WPA of the 1930s, and Bellevue Hospital, as well as a biography of Jane Addams, an historical atlas of American women's history, and several co-authored books and articles on social policy. She worked for a number of years at Hudson River Psychiatric Center, and later taught American History and Urban History at Bard, Vassar, and Marist Colleges. She serves as an occasional lecturer at the Center for Lifetime Studies.

Melodye K. Moore is head of the Collections Committee of the Dutchess County Historical Society and serves as a Trustee on the Board. She is a past recipient of the Helen Wilkinson Reynolds Award from the society. From 1979 to 1986, Moore served as director of DCHS, before taking on the job of managing all site operations at the Staatsburgh State Historic Site (Mills Mansion). Since her retirement from directing the Mills Mansion, she has returned to DCHS as a trustee in 2011.

Camille Roccanova is a cultural institutions and libraries planning strategist. A Hudson Valley native, she now lives in the northwest corner of Connecticut. She holds a B.A. in Visual Art from Bennington College and an MLIS from Simmons University.

Dutchess County Historical Society Vice Presidents Representing the Cities and Towns of the County

In 2018, we put in place the full restoration of the long-held tradition of having "local" Vice Presidents who act in a non-executive capacity. They are a single point of contact for the cities, towns, and villages across the county. They might address county-wide issues such as determining how best to obtain and share stories of our veterans. Or they might address a unique or one-off need. Franklin D. Roosevelt served as DCHS Vice President for Hyde Park from 1926 until his death.

Amenia: Julian Strauss

Beacon: Theresa Kraft

Beekman: *Vacant*

Clinton: Craig Marshall

Dover: Caroline Reichenberg and Valerie Larobardier

East Fishkill: Rick Soedler

Fishkill: Joey Cavaccini

Hyde Park: Shannon Butler

Lagrange: *Vacant*

Milan: Victoria LoBrutto

Washington & Millbrook: Jim Inglis

North East & Millerton: Ed Downey & Jane Rossman

Pawling: *Vacant*

Pine Plains: Dyan Wapnick

Pleasant Valley: Dieter Friedrichsen

Poughkeepsie: *Vacant*

Red Hook: Emily Majer

Rhinebeck Town & Village: Michael Frazier & David Miller

Stanford: Kathy Spiers

Union Vale: Fran Wallin

Wappingers: Joey Cavaccini

DCHS Donors

Supporters August 2018 to August 2019

$1,000 & Above

Absolute Auctions & Realty, Inc.

Adams Fairacre Farms

Doris Adams

Anonymous, Community Foundations of the Hudson Valley

Ronald R. & Betsy Atkins

Central Hudson Gas & Electric,

Martin & Eleanor Charwat

Cogent Communications

Lillian Cumming Fund, Rhode Island Community Foundation

D'Arcangelo & Co., LLP

National Society Daughters of the American Revolution

Frank Doherty

Downey, Haab, & Murphy, PLLC

Rob & Susan Doyle

John & Gloria Golden

Julius & Carla Gude

Shirley Handel

Ronald Huber

Hudson Views

Hudson River Valley Institute

Denise Lawlor Fund

Lou & Candace Lewis

Mahwenawasigh Chapter NSDAR

Marist College

Marshall & Sterling, Inc.

Melodye Moore & Lenny Miller

Poughkeepsie Public Library District

Poughkeepsie Rural Cemetery

Louis M. Salerno

Joan Smith

Elizabeth & Julian Strauss

Wilson Foundation

Zimmer Brothers Jewelers

Andrew Zobler & Manny Urquiza

$100 to $999

Susan Adams

Christine Altavilla

Myra Young Armstead

John & Anne Atherton

Babiarz Court Reporting Service, Inc.

Harry Baldwin

Richard Birch

Michael Boden

Mary Brockway

J. Vincent Buck

Peter Bunten

Melanie Cancellari

Miriam Cohen

John Conklin

Christine Crawford-Oppenheimer

CR Properties Group LLC

Edward & Margaretta Downey

Dutchess Community College

Jack & Rita Effron.

Amy R. & Steven L. Effron,

Eugene Fleishman & Judith Elkin

Peter & Anne Forman

Joanna Frang & Mark Debald

Nancy Fogel

Michael & Cecily Frazier

Russ Frehling & Debra Blalock

Gellert Family Donor Advised Fund

Arthur Gellert

Brian Gerber

Jack & Fredrica Goodman

Edith Greenwood

Eileen & Benjamin Hayden

H D L Associates Inc

Health Quest Systems Inc.

Ann Hector

E. Stuart & Linda Hubbard

Michael Jacoff & Jeanne Vanecko

William Jeffway & Christopher Lee

Rev. Tyler & Mary Jones

Bradford & Barbara Kendall

Betsy Kopstein-Stuts

Peter Krulewitch
Virginia LaFalce
Karen Lambdin
Steven & Linda Lant
Tom Lawrence
Edwin Leonard
Lewis & Greer, P.C.
Roderick Link
Victoria Lobrutto
David Lund
Craig Marshall
Antonia L. Mauro,
Robert & Patricia McAlpine
Joseph McGowan
Mount Gulian
Kathleen Moyer
John Mylod
James & Margaret Nelson
David Nicholls
Philip Peters
Michael A. & Patricia L. Prunty
Eileen & Denny Quinn
Viggo Rambusch
Real Property Abstract & Title
Services, LLC
Caroline Reichenberg
Arthur Rollin
Albert & Julia Rosenblatt

Salisbury Bank
Andres San Millan
David Schwartz
Shawangunk Valley Conservancy
Joan Smith
Elizabeth Smith
Nevill & Karen Smythe
Warren Becket Soule
Paul Sparrow
Werner Steger
Stoutenburgh Teller Family
Association
Mark Tallardy
William P. Tatum III
Teahan & Constantino LLP
Sandra Tunstill
Patricia Turner
Van Dewater & Van Dewater, LLP
Peter Van Kleeck
Jeanne Vanecko
Phillip K. & Barbara L. Vanitallie
Mary Jane and Ron Von Allmen
Reginald Ward
Mary Westermann
Janna & Carlos Whearty,
Elizabeth Mylod Wolf
Vanessa Young
Andrew Villani

Under $100

Virginia Augerson
Stuart Baker
Deborah A. Barber
Carlyle Black
Joan & Charles Blanksteen

Ellen Chase
Edward Cigna
Joanne Clarke
Natalie Condon
Fred Couse

Dennis & Susan Creegan

Jeff Cronk

Donald J. Delaney

John Desmond

Chez & Roseanne Di Gregorio

Michael Dolan

John & Abby Dux

Andrew & Barbara Effron

Debra & Robert Erickson

Stephen Fiore

Edwin Fitchett

Gail Fitzpatrick-Fox

Stephen & Anne Friedland

Dieter Friedrichsen

Nancy & Mark Giordano

Michael & Deborah Gordon

Nancy Greer

Sarah Hermans

Victor & Patricia Hilts

Graham Jones

Justin Kemp

Michael & Roseann Kemp

UNDER $100

Sean Klay

Claudine & Christoper Klose

Lawrence Laliberte

Peter & Diane Lapis

Rev. Canon James Elliott Lindsley

Lainie Lobus

Stephen Lumb

Kay Macke

Lawrence Magill

Robert Magill

Cora Mallory-Davis

David Marshall

Zinas Mavodones

Gail & Thomas McGlinchey

Lori Morritt

North East Historical Society

Sandra Opdycke

Matthew Pastre

Susan Pianka

Barbara Post

William Rhoads

Douglas & Michele Rofrano

Diane & Randy Rogers

Janice Selag

Ann Shershin

Doris Sieck Dubac

Richard Soedler

Marguerite Spratt

Stanford Historical Society

Craig Strauss

Three Arts Bookstore

Barbara Tiger

Joan Traver

Frank Van Zanten

Nancy VanCoughnett

Richard & Ellen Wager

Frances Wallin

Ann Wentworth

Richard Wiedeman

Michael Williams

Elizabeth Wolf

Bonnie Wood

Lifetime Members

Herman Harmelink

Homeland Foundation

Michael Levin

Lou & Candace Lewis

Zinas Mavadones

W.P. McDermott

Melodye Moore & Lenny Miller

Harold Nestler

Sheila Newman

Joan Sherman

Paul South

Norma Shirley

C. B. Spross

Peter & Myna VanKleeck

William Wade

The Society encourages the use of memorial donations to remember a loved one, or the gift of a special donation in honor of one's birthday, anniversary, or special occasion. Please be assured that all such remembrances will be appropriately acknowledged with a special letter from the Society expressing our sincerest thanks.

It has been the policy of the Dutchess County Historical Society to print only the categories seen above due to space limitations. We certainly value all of our member and donors, including Lifetime, Individual, Family, and Organization. We appreciate each and every one of you. Thank you for your continued support as we move forward into our second one hundred years.

Directory of Dutchess County Municipal Historians and Historical Societies

Prepared by William P. Tatum III, Ph.D.

Updated July 19, 2019
To update this directory, contact County Historian Will Tatum below.

DUTCHESS COUNTY HISTORIAN

William P. Tatum III
22 Market Street, Poughkeepsie, New York 12601
(845) 486-2381   fax (845) 486-2138
wtatum@dutchessny.gov

DUTCHESS COUNTY HISTORICAL SOCIETY

Bill Jeffway, *Executive Director*
Post Office Box 88, Poughkeepsie, New York 12602
(845) 471-1630
bill.jeffway@dchsny.org

CITY HISTORIANS / HISTORICAL SOCIETIES

Beacon Post Office Box 89, Beacon, New York 12508
Historian: Robert Murphy info@beaconhistorical.org
Tel: (845) 831-1514
Historical Society: Diane Lapis dlapis@beaconhistorical.org
beaconhistorical.org (845) 831-0514

Poughkeepsie 93 Market Street, Poughkeepsie, New York 12601
Historian: Tom Lawrence tlawrence@poklib.org 845-485-3445 x 3306

TOWN & VILLAGE HISTORIANS / HISTORICAL SOCIETIES

Amenia Amenia Town Hall, 4988 Route 22, Amenia, New York 12501
   Historian: *Vacant*
   Historical Society: Betsy Strauss strausshouse72@gmail.com
   Post Office Box 22, Amenia, New York 12501

Beekman 4 Main Street, Poughquag, New York 12570
  Historian: Patricia Goewey
  Tel: (845) 724-5300

Clinton 820 Fiddlers Bridge Road, Rhinebeck, New York 12572
  Historian: Craig Marshall craigmarshall266@aol.com
  (845) 242-5879
  Historical Society: Cynthia Koch cynthiakoch@optonline.net
  clintonhistoricalsociety.org
  Post Office Box 122, Clinton Corners, New York 12514

Dover 126 East Duncan Hill Road, Dover Plains, New York 12522
  Historian: Valerie Larobardier valarobardier@gmail.com
  (845) 849-6025
  Historian: Caroline Reichenberg sweetcaroliner@aol.com
  Historical Society: Fran Braley alfranb@optonline.net
  (845) 832-7949
  180 Old State Route 22, Dover Plains NY 12522

East Fishkill Post Office Box 245, Hopewell Junction, New York 12533
  Historian: David Koehler healthyharvestcsa@gmail.com
  (845) 226-8877
  Historical Society: Rick Soedler rjsoedler@gmail.com
  (845) 227-5374

Fishkill (Town) Fishkill Town Hall, 807 NY Route 52, Fishkill, NY 12524
  Historian: Paul Gromkowski
  (845) 831-7800 Ext. 3309
  Historical Society: Steve Lynch asklynch@yahoo.com
  (914) 525-7667
  Post Office Box 133, Fishkill, New York 12524

Fishkill (Village) 1140 Main Street, Fishkill, New York 12524
  Historian: Allan Way allanway2@aol.com 845-896-9696

Hyde Park 4383 Albany Post Road, Hyde Park, New York 12538
  Historian: Shannon Butler rangerbutler.sb@gmail.com
  Historical Society: Patsy Costello patsyc97@aol.com (845) 229-2559
  Post Office Box 182, Hyde Park, New York 12538

LaGrange Post Office Box 112, LaGrangeville, New York 12540
  Historian: Georgia Trott-Herring herringtrott@aol.com
  (845) 452-2911
  Historical Society: Bob D'Amato
  lagrangehistoricalsociety@gmail.com (845) 489-5183

Milan Milan Town Hall, 20 Wilcox Circle, Milan, New York 12571
Historian: Vicky LoBrutto victorialobrutto@gmail.com

Millbrook (Village) Washington (Town)
Historian: David Greenwood ngreenwd@aol.com (845) 677-5767
3248 Sharon Turnpike, Millbrook, New York 12545
Historical Society: Robert McHugh computermail@msn.com
Post Office Box 135, Millbrook, New York 12545

Millerton / Northeast
Historian (Town): Lisa Cope northeasttown@taconic.net
(518) 789-3300 ext 603
PO Box 516, Millerton, NY 12546
Historical Society: Ed Downey eddowney@millertonlawyer.com
(518) 789-4442
Post Office Box 727, Millerton, New York 12546

Pawling (Historical Society of Quaker Hill and Pawling)
Historian (Town): Robert Reilly sc31redsky@gmail.com
(845) 855-5040
160 Charles Colman Blvd, Pawling, New York 12564
Historian (Village): *Vacant*
Historical Society: Jaclyn Wagner pawlinghistory@gmail.com
Post Office Box 99, Pawling, New York 12564

Pine Plains
Historian: *Vacant*
Historical Society: Dyan Wapnick dyan.wapnick@gmail.com
(518) 398-5344
Post Office Box 243, Pine Plains, New York 12567
Dutchess County Historical Society VP: Dyan Wapnick
dyan.wapnick@gmail.com

Pleasant Valley
Historian: Fred Schaeffer fredinhv@aol.com (845) 454-1190
1544 Main Street (Route 44), Pleasant Valley, New York 12569
Historical Society: Mary Ellen Cowles merc@hvc.rr.com
DCHS VP: Marilyn Bradford momof5ny@yahoo.com
(845) 518-0998

Poughkeepsie (Town)
Historian: John R. Pinna townhistorian@townofpoughkeepsie-ny.gov
(845) 485-3646
1 Overrocker Road, Poughkeepsie, New York 12603

Red Hook

Historian (Town): Emily Majer emily.majer@gmail.com
7340 South Broadway, Red Hook, New York 12571
Historian (Village): Sally Dwyer-McNulty
sally.dwyer-mcnulty@marist.edu
7467 South Broadway, Red Hook, New York 12571
Historical Society: Claudine Klose claudineklose@gmail.com
(845) 758-1920
Post Office Box 397, Red Hook, New York 12571

Rhinebeck

Historian (Town): Nancy Kelly kinship@hvc.rr.com (845) 876-4592
Historian (Village): Michael Frazier michaelfrazier@earthlink.net
(845) 876-7462
Historical Society: David Miller dhmny@aol.com (845) 750-4486
Post Office Box 291, Rhinebeck, New York 12572

Stanford

Historian: Kathy Spiers lakeendinn@aol.com (845) 868-7320
Historical Society: Kathy Spiers
Post Office Box 552, Bangall, New York 12506

Tivoli

Historian: Gregory B. Moynahan, Ph.D. moynahan@bard.edu
Post Office Box 5000, Annandale-on-Hudson, New York 12504-5000

Unionvale

Historian: Fran Wallin franw821@hotmail.com
Town Office (845) 724-5600
249 Duncan Road, Lagrangeville, New York 12540
Historical Society: Peter Gay (Vice President) chargaysgy@gmail.com
(845)-677-4837

Wappinger/Wappingers Falls

Town Historian: Joey Cavacinni jcavaccini@townofwappinger.us
Town Office (845) 297-4158 ext 107
Town Hall: 20 Middle Bush Road, Wappingers Falls, NY 12590
Village Historian: Brenda VonBurg (845) 297-2697
Historical Society: Beth Devine info@wappingershistorialsociety.org
(845) 430-9520
Post Office Box 174, Wappinger Falls, New York 12590

Dutchess County Historical Society

P.O. Box 88
Poughkeepsie, NY 12602
845-471-1630
DCHSNY.org
contact@dchsny.org

JOIN AS A MEMBER

Throughout the year, the Dutchess County Historical Society offers exhibitions, talks, and workshops on a broad array of topics.

Help support the work of the Society.

MISSION STATEMENT AND GOALS

The Society is a not-for-profit educational organization that collects, preserves, and interprets the history of Dutchess County, New York, from the period of the arrival of the first Native Americans until the present day.

Furthermore, The Society aims:

- To collect, catalogue, and preserve artifacts that make visual and tangible connections to the history of Dutchess County.

- To create permanent and temporary exhibitions, programs, and publications to stimulate interest in the history of Dutchess County.

- To develop program partnerships with other historical, educational, and governmental groups to promote community involvement with the history of Dutchess County.

- To serve the needs of researchers, educators, students, DCHS members, and members of the general public who wish to study and use the collection.

LEVELS OF MEMBERSHIP

Individual $35
Includes free library access and a complimentary copy of the DCHS Yearbook. Early notice, special invitation to programs and events, and recognition in the Yearbook.

Associate Membership.......$20
You get full Individual Membership benefits, at a special price. Reserved for those with a paid membership in a city, town or village historical society. Effectively a benefit of local historical society membership.

Family/Contributor.............$50
Includes all of the above for family.

Sustaining..........................$100
*Includes all of the above, and your choice of any back-issue Yearbook
where we have inventory.*

Patron $250
*Includes above, and your choice of any two back-issues of our
Yearbook where we have inventory.*

Sponsor..............................$500
*Includes above, and your choice of any of our own (DCHS) published
books where inventory allows.*

Millennial Circle $1,000
*Includes above with 2 tickets to Annual Awards Galaand/or
a summary research topic of your choice.*

JOIN DCHS TODAY!

Millennial Circle $1,000
Sponsor..............................$500
Patron $250
Sustaining..........................$100
Family/Contributor.............$50
Individual $35
Associate $20
Additional Gift...................$_____

Dutchess County Historical Society

Total $ _____

You may send a check to DCHS, P.O. Box 88, Poughkeepsie, NY, 12602
or join online at DCHSNY.org/membership.

Name

Address

City   State   Zip

Phone   email